# The Tangram Method

**Fostering self-awareness in neurodivergent young people through conversation**

*Hilra Gondim Vinha, PhD*

# The Tangram Method

**Fostering self-awareness in neurodivergent young people through conversation**

*Hilra Gondim Vinha, PhD*

Copyright © 2022 Hilra Gondim Vinha, PhD

All rights reserved. No part of this book may be reproduced in any form or by any electronic or mechanical means, including information storage and retrieval systems, without permission in writing from the author, except by reviewers, who may quote brief passages in a review.

ISBN: 978-1-80352-126-8 (Paperback)

ISBN: 978-1-80352-127-5 (Hardback)

Printed in Great Britain

Publisher: Independent Publishing Network

First publication date: 25 August 2022

This edition: 26 September 2024

Author: Hilra Gondim Vinha, PhD

Website: **hilravinha.com**

Email: **tangram@hilravinha.com**

illustrations:

Weaver Lima @**weaverlima**

Ana Beatriz Benigno @**MAGIKKA.carrd.co** @**oomagika**

*Please direct all inquiries to the author.*

*To Sessé*

# Contents

**Introduction to the second edition 11**

**Foreword 13**

**Preface 15**

**The research 19**

*The young people behind the fictional characters 20*

*A glimpse of the fictionalised story 21*

**The autism awareness programme 35**

*Characters inspired by real young people 36*

**The approach before the method 69**

*The Relate model: the starting point 74*

*Coaching and the 'Thinking' stage 76*

**The Tangram Method 85**

*Learning from their stories 86*

**Takeaways 99**

*Putting it into practice 100*

*Strategies for the seven principles 104*

*The talking principle with the overly talkative 104*

*The talking principle with the less verbal 105*

*How to implement the other principles 106*

*The neurodiversity cards 110*

**Shared resources 125**

*Improving social skills and avoiding masking 129*

*How to use the neurodiversity awareness card game 131*

## Extended resources and final thoughts 149

*Materials available via Inclusive Thoughts 150*

*Supplementary resources 150*

*Some earlier publications 151*

*A final thought 153*

## Acknowledgements 155

## References and further reading 159

*References 159*

*Further reading 160*

*In memoriam*

In loving memory of the most devoted and inspiring reader I have ever known, my mother.

# Introduction to the second edition

This book was first published in 2022; and I was all set to celebrate its completion with a wonderful launch event surrounded by close friends and family. However, plans changed when some important questions popped up about the informed consent from the individuals whose stories inspired the method and the book itself. Even though the consent was ethically sound; and I had already anonymised the real individuals by fictionalising and mixing up their stories, I was advised to go the extra mile in protecting the contributors' identities, which I gladly did.

I want to assure you that no personal data was used in the telling of these stories or in any part of this book. The stories that inspired the characters and the creation of the method come from neurodivergent individuals who are now fully grown adults. They are passionate about sharing their experiences to help young people on their journey toward strengthening their identity and sense of self.

This second edition comes after much reflection and growth. It represents a stronger conviction that this method is truly useful. It plays a vital role in helping allies and advocates empower neurodivergent individuals to be their authentic selves, free from masking and silencing.

# Foreword

Jackie Smith

My son Tom was blessed the day he met Hilra, for here was a lady who would change his life. Not only was she able to tune in to him and help him understand himself, but she was also able to help his school understand his needs and make adjustments to enable him to continue in education. Before she came along, his education had been sporadic. He had had a few good teaching assistants in the past, but they were unable to influence any changes that made a difference to him accessing education.

It was not easy for Hilra as she had to gain Tom's trust and find out what made him uncomfortable (which is no easy task for a confused neurodivergent young person). This had to be done in order to make the necessary alterations to his school days.

Hilra arranged weekly visits to a local university, she arranged for Tom to work outside the classroom if he felt unable to attend a lesson; she also arranged for different methods of communication if he felt unable to voice his frustrations. These small changes made a huge difference and made it possible for him to stay in education.

Not only was Tom blessed, but our whole family were, as we could relax knowing Tom had the support he needed to allow the education he deserved. We are eternally grateful to Hilra for she was a strong role model, who helped to shape the amazing young man he is today.

This book is amazing. I am confident it will help people to realise that their traits not only do not need to control their lives, but also they can help other people understand how to adapt their own behaviour which would, in turn, enable these young people to grow and survive the educational system.

Jackie Smith is a parent and unwavering champion of neurodiversity. She lent her invaluable support to the embryonic activities that laid the foundations of the Tangram Method.

# Preface

Learning connects me with my roots and beginnings, while storytelling connects me with others. This book explores the stories of people I encountered, connected with and learned from. It is an invitation to connect. I tell what I have learned working with some extraordinary young people over the years, in hope that you will learn from them too. Firstly, my younger brother José (also known by the nickname Sessé). As an infant he was labelled 'exceptional' by medical professionals. At the time, this was an alternative word used in Brazil to describe a child with a learning disability, in an attempt to avoid stigmatising and diminishing. Sessé was believed to have autism and developmental delay, described to my parents as a mismatch between chronological and cognitive age. It was with my brother that I learned my first lessons on the meanings of being *different* and not meeting societal expectations.

Secondly, my pupils taught me immensely when I was a primary school teacher. I learned incredible things with them. Being their teacher impacted the professional I became and, years later, shaped my research project. The dialogical pedagogy I fostered with my pupils has remained a guiding principle in any work I have done with young people since, including years later when interviewing for my research.

In the first chapter of this book, I introduce some of the participants whose stories gave colour and shape to my thesis (which some may say resembles a graphic novel more than a doctoral report). Participants created self-portraits using the cut-out paper body parts created for the research data collection. I then turned their stories into fiction and gave them new names to protect their identities. You can find a small sample of that fiction in the first chapter of this book.

In later chapters, I share my conversations with young people about their experiences of autism. I tell the story of how I took stock of what I learned from and with them to create the Tangram Method. I introduce seven characters inspired by experts by experience, whose stories are the foundations of the method. The stories give insight into autism and its many facets and various divergent outlooks.

**Language disclaimer**

The terminologies I use in this book correspond to the preferred language of the young people whose stories I share. They did not use the identity 'person with autism' favouring 'autistic person'. I also refer to Asperger's when mentioning an earlier diagnosis as this was the term used at the time.

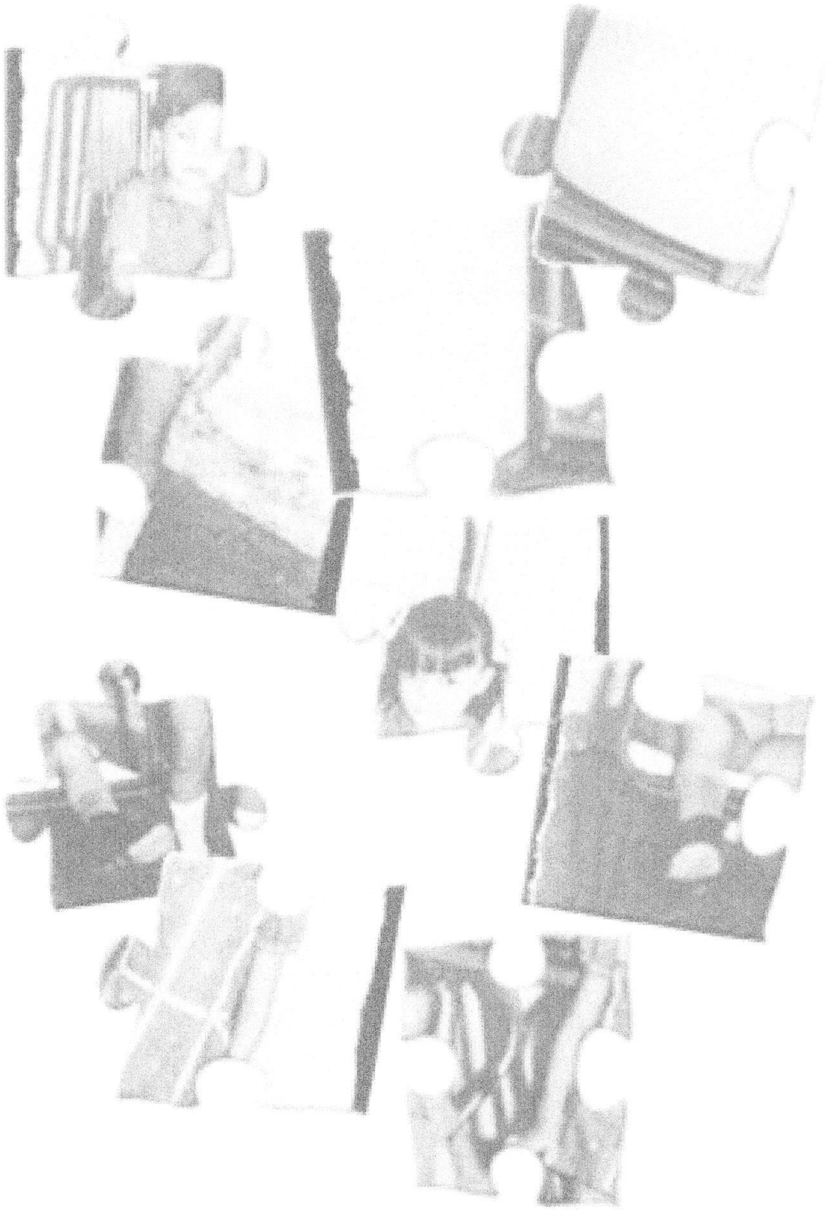

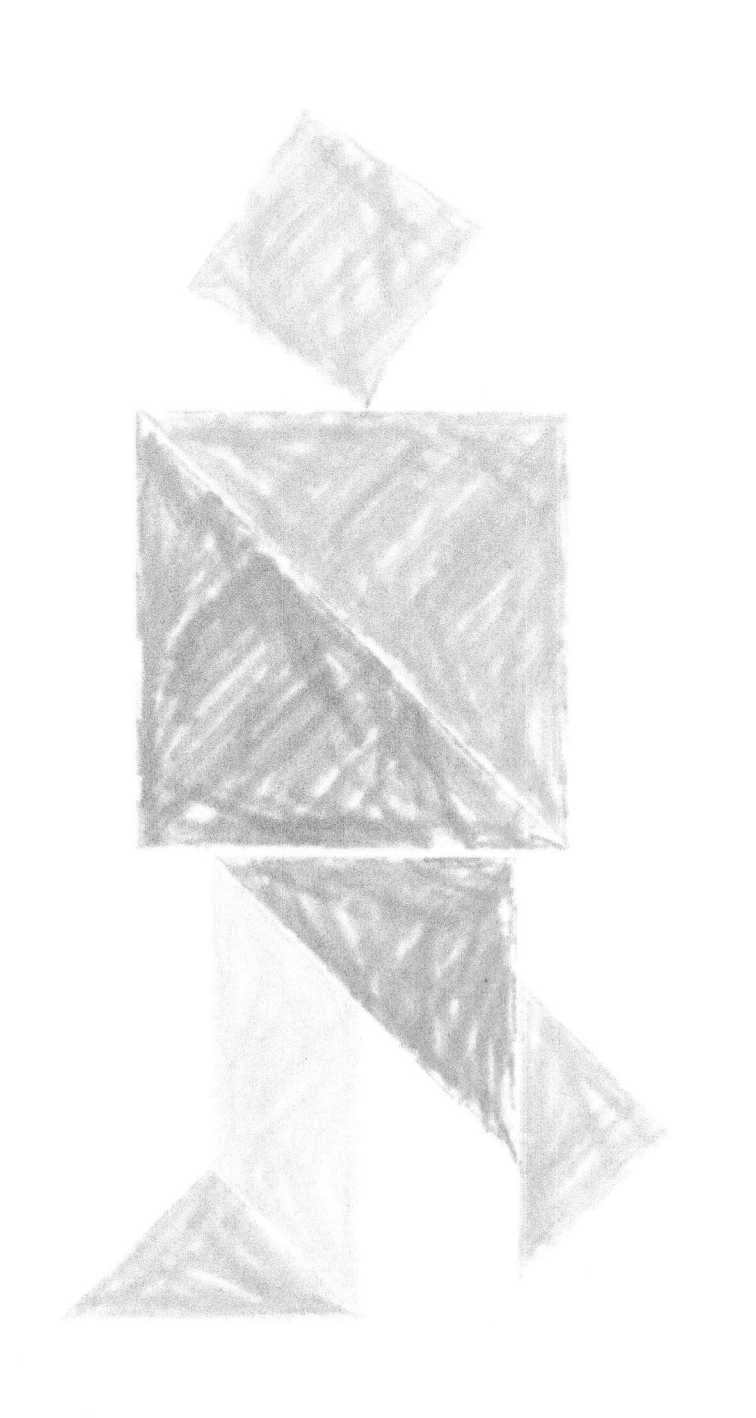

# The research

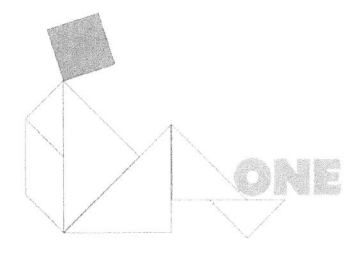

My research was about how learners in mainstream settings represent people with a learning disability, in comparison to those in special schools. To capture their views, I used pictures of body parts created especially for the study, which the participants used to build self-portraits and portraits of people they knew. They produced an intriguing collection of images showing how they perceived people with a learning disability.

From my conversations with these young people, I wrote a fictionalised story and included it in my thesis. I created fictional characters based on the participants; and I used the transcripts from interviews to build the narrative. I used their portraits combined with their verbal and nonverbal cues to create two short graphic episodes inside the story. Next, I introduce the young people who inspired the story. I gave them nicknames to protect their identity. Immediately after introducing the participants, I share the fictionalised episode, *Encounters*, which is an abridged extract from my thesis.

# The young people behind the fictional characters

## Carl

*he/him/his*

Carl was fourteen and attended a special school when I met him. He was autistic and described himself as an artist. Carl told me he did not like copying anyone's creations, preferring to produce his own. All pictures that Carl created of himself with the paper body parts had only a head and legs. However, when picturing other people, Carl included other body parts.

## Lynne

*she/her/hers*

Lynne was also fourteen and was Carl's best friend. They attended the same special school. Lynne was not autistic and had speech, language and communication difficulties, yet she was talkative.

Lynne was always accompanied by her teaching assistant Mrs Bell. Mrs Bell constantly interrupted Lynne to correct her posture, the placement of her hands or what she was saying. Fortunately, on the occasions that Mrs Bell left the room for a brief period, Lynne would make the most of the time and speak freely. All of Lynne's self-portraits had separated parts (except the ones Mrs Bell 'corrected'). Even when asked to hand draw herself, Lynne drew a body with disconnected parts. Only when picturing other people did Lynne join the body parts together.

## Alicia

*she/her/hers*

Alicia was autistic and was thirteen at the time. She attended a mainstream school, while her younger sister who was also autistic attended a special school. I interviewed both sisters and their mother. The younger sister did not engage much in the interviews, only saying she wanted to have friends, but the other children were unkind to her. Alicia in contrast, spoke profusely about school and her pictures were realistic.

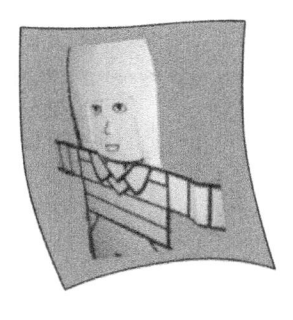

## Jay

*she/her/hers*

Jay represents a child with Down syndrome who attended the same special school as Alicia's sister; she visited the family during one of my interviews. Jay was not part of the study but I created a character to represent Jay because of the disturbing names the younger sister called her.

# A glimpse of the fictionalised story

*Encounters* is a shortened version of that fictionalised story. Through the narrative I told the stories of what those young people shared in the interviews and included some interactions I had with the adults working with them, such as Lynne's teaching assistant. The fictionalised device allowed me to bring to light some of my feelings, impressions and thought processes, which in a formal research report are typically expected to be left out. The fictionalised story also permitted me to keep the tradition of including my brother. He appears as the visitor to whom I introduce my fictional neighbours (the young people in my research) and I also share some of the emotions that emerged from my conversations with them.

**The Tangram Method**

# Encounters

# The research

I had come a long way before moving to this neighbourhood where I live. What once was strange is now my familiar ground. Today, I belong here, though part of me will always be rooted far away. Hence my delight whenever a breeze from my old home reaches me. Like when I received a letter from my mother telling me my brother was coming.

> Dear daughter,
>
> I'm delighted to tell you that your baby brother will be visiting you soon! He will stay for a week, and I'm certain it will be a delightful time for both of you. He misses you dearly every day, and your unique ability to understand and communicate with him is truly irreplaceable. He's also eager to meet your friends during his stay. I kindly ask you to gently remind him that his visit is temporary, and he will need to bid farewell and return home soon. You understand his need for preparation before any changes occur.
>
> love,
> Mum

## The Tangram Method

Weeks after that letter, my brother arrived and with him came a nostalgia from my childhood. He also brought the laughter that always made me happy and the eyes which guided me wherever I went. We started visiting my beloved neighbours, beginning with Carl.

I explained to Sessé that Carl had learning difficulties and attended a special school. But I did not need to say all these words. All I had to say was,

'We will see Carl. He is CR'.

Sessé uses CR as a shorthand for the special school he attended as a child (the school was known by the acronym ABCR). For him, CR also means someone with learning difficulties or a physical disability.

We knocked at Carl's house and, like magic, we went inside. Carl said hello and introduced us to his family and friends.

2

The research

We said we had to go and meet other friends, which saddened Carl as he could not come with us. We understood his sadness. We knew the gloom of hopelessness too well. He had learned to get over it and move on. As we did.

The second visit was incredibly intriguing, as we knocked at an unusual house. There were tags, labels and signs all over the front façade. These tags had words printed on them. My brother could not read, so I had to read those words aloud, which was excruciating for us. I read in a murmur 's**z' and 'r*t**d'. My voice trembled when I said the last word after so many years of silencing it from my memories. That was the most painful word of our childhood and probably the most frequently used.

I had just finished reading that excruciating last word when a little blonde girl wearing huge glasses opened the door. Sessé whispered towards me,

'She is CR.'

# The research

She was wearing a school uniform with more tags and labels. I was relieved that my brother did not ask me to read these labels, instead he was curious about why she had them. She answered timidly,

'I don't know. I have been carrying them since I can remember. I feel like they are part of me. Besides, people stick new ones on all the time.'

We all sighed simultaneously, as she continued,

'My Mum helps me remove some of the labels from time to time. But some are well glued on and we are not sure if we can ever get rid of them'.

We all sighed again. Next, she showed us a tiny golden tag that she loved. It was the smallest of them all and sat underneath all the other labels, hence us not noticing it at first. In beautiful handwriting, it read 'Jay'. With a sparkle in her eyes, she declared,

'That is me. I am Jay. My mum made that one for me'.

That visit was unsettling for both of us, because Sessé and I knew those hurtful words just too well and also had struggled trying to get rid of them. We wanted to give Jay hope, but we were old enough to know that some labels stay for life and others hurt long after they are gone.

After remembering all those words, we needed some time to process our emotions. We sat down and watched TV, just like in the old days. My brother was never able to speak much, but we did not need the words that he could not articulate. They were not necessary just now. We understood each other's sadness beyond words.

The next day, I took my brother to see one of my favourite neighbours, Lynne. People sometimes needed Carl's help to understand Lynne's words. Carl and Lynne were best friends. Seeing Carl and Lynne together always reminded me of our childhood, when I helped people understand Sessé.

6

The research

# LYNNE

| | | |
|---|---|---|
| I'M GLAD YOU ARE HERE. IT'S SO NICE TO MEET YOU. | I TRIED TO SAY SOMETHING BUT NO ONE LISTENS TO ME. | I'M NOT A LITTLE BABY. |
| I'M BECOMING A LADY. LET ME SHOW YOU A PICTURE OF ME. | SEE? THESE ARE MY BOOBIES. I'M NOT A BABY. | ROGER LIKES ME, HE DOES. HE IS IN MY CLASS. |
| THIS IS MY DAD. I DON'T LIKE WHEN HE COMES TO MY SCHOOL. DO I, DAD? | THAT'S MY MUM. YOU CAN'T SEE HER, CAN YOU? SHE'S SOMEWHERE. | SO YOU HAVE TO GO NOW, DO YOU? I HOPE YOU COME ANOTHER DAY. |

7

We were listening to Lynne when we heard something like a doorbell,

'Ring, ring, what do you need to do next?'.

That was strange, a speaking doorbell. Lynne seemed to know what to do, so she grabbed a chair for us with her usual large smile. She was about to say something when the bell rang again,

'Ring, ring, first let them sit down, then you can have a chat. What do you need to do next?'

Lynne did not say anything but pointed at the chair and waited for us to sit. She then covered her mouth with one hand when trying to say something. The bell interrupted again,

'Ring, ring! Put your hand down, sit properly, then we can understand what you are saying. What do you need to do next?'

She sat with both hands under her knees, keeping her whole body together. Then, she spoke slowly to ensure she was saying the right words:

'Natalie does not like me. She always says bad things about me'.

Lynne started saying more when we heard the bell again:

'Ring! ring! You are not supposed to talk about Natalie with your visitors. That is our business only. What do you need to do next?'.

After leaving Lynne's house, we went for a walk in the park because we needed some fresh air. We played children's games. We laughed, we ran my brother's little slow-galloping run, he flapped his hands many times with joy and we finally sat down to rest a little.

9

After the park, we went to see Alicia because she had always been joyful and keen to meet new friends. I knew she would cheer us up, as she did. Alicia received us with friendly hugs and, before we left, we sang together 'You have a friend in me'.

The days with my brother had been precious, but the time for him to leave was approaching. We visited all my neighbours; Sessé now knew all my new friends, just like in the old days. When the time came to say our farewells, we both knew the distance would never keep us apart, because we have always carried each other inside, everywhere we went.

10

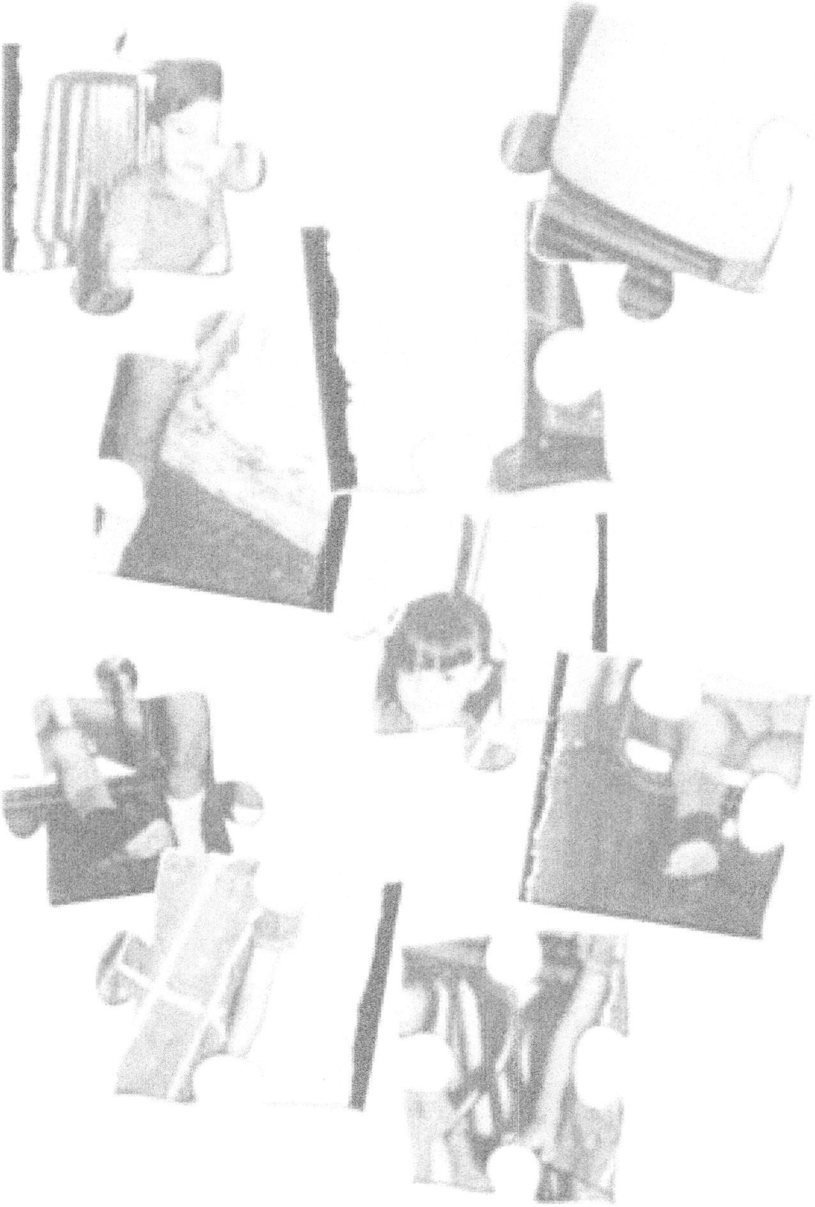

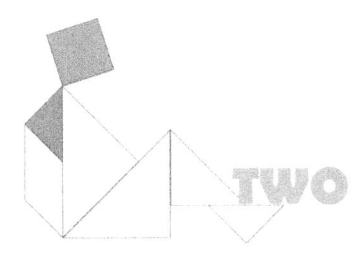

# The autism awareness programme

He looked at me with a timid smile and said:

>'You scare me, Miss.'

I smiled back, unsure why I scared him. The following day, when he walked past me, he said again,

>'You scare me, Miss.' And he gave me a wider smile.

I realised this was his way of greeting me. That greeting became a ritual in which he acknowledged me and repeated the sentence he found so funny. One day, I instinctively asked,

>'But why?' and he replied grinning again,

>'Because you do.'

That became the new ritual. Terence would say I scared him, I would ask why and he would say because I did. I am not sure how long that interaction pattern lasted or how we progressed from that, but eventually, we started talking in a way resembling a dialogue, a chat of some sort. The transition from the ritual of pseudo-dialogue to the actual conversation seemed natural, although the taste for teasing never left him.

Sometime later in the year, I started supporting Terence outside lessons and became his main point of contact at school. I was involved in all meetings regarding his learning and met with his parents, who told me he had a diagnosis of Asperger's. They did not know how to support him and hoped I could help, as I seemed to know about autism and had a good rapport with him. I clarified that I had a good understanding of learning difficulties and some presentation of autism, but I could not claim to be well informed about Asperger's or high functioning autism. Nonetheless, I was keen to help if I could, as I had no problems communicating with Terence or understanding his ways of thinking. We shared the same sense of humour and could share a giggle about the silliest of things.

Soon after, I organised a weekly meeting with Terence. These were the first autism awareness sessions I had ever done and the beginning of the story that this book tells. The whole story is a reflection of the conversations I had with young people I met over the past ten years who wanted to talk about their school experiences and how they related to and communicated with others.

Many of these conversations were unplanned or occasional and some became regular. Each young person who engaged in conversation gave me insight into their expertise in their experience with autism in the neurotypical world.

## Characters inspired by real young people

Those young people are embodied in the seven protagonists, but each representing predominantly a young person I met in real life, they are not direct depictions, due to fictionalised key elements of their story that protect their identity, while still presenting their autistic experiences with real-life insights and reflections. The fictionalised elements are aspects inherited from multiple neurodivergent young people who engaged in the emergence of the Tangram Method. Those individuals were significantly different from each other and each had distinct goals and motivations for our conversations, hence all the different formats, timings and activities I used together with the need to adapt, change and innovate constantly. However, there are several similarities in their journeys, the barriers they faced and the way the method adjusted to each one of them.

## Terence

*he/him/his*

When I first met Terence, he used to leave the classroom without asking permission, often missing essential pieces of information. Terence described the reason for his little escapades as getting overwhelmed with a topic and scared to ask the teacher to explain it again.

Terence was fourteen years old like everyone else, but had a passion for high-quality vintage, old-fashioned stuff, including music from the 1930s.

## The beginning

Terence explained that the reason for his difficulties to remain in the classroom for the duration of a lesson was his autism. Intrigued by his statement, I asked how autism caused the struggle. He did not know. I said I would love to understand that better and asked if he would like to learn more about it as well, so we could have a regular meeting to talk about it. He agreed to try because he had appreciated our discussions so far.

## The book

After I had met with his parents, I conducted some research and acquired a book written for teenagers (Grossberg, 2012) to make sense of school and friends. The book was an excellent resource that included accessible information about autism and several writing activities. Terence started by completing a little test about feelings and emotions. Answering to one of the questions, he responded that he did not recognise when he was distressed in a lesson until he had to leave.

Once completing the test, we talked about other emotions he had experienced in life and which situations would cause a similar reaction. We spent several sessions on Chapter 2, about learning to identify emotions: understanding what you feel; listening to your body; understanding how other people think; ranking your problems; decoding fears; dealing with change; getting upset in class; knowing when you need a break; and getting help. Those conversations became a significant part of the process toward autism awareness and the main focus of our sessions in the first term.

Terence had a strong bond with his parents, especially his father, with whom he shared several special interests such as antiques. He was also very close to his grandmother, with whom he spent many weekends attending car boot fairs and other treasure hunt events. Terence could articulate how he felt when doing stuff with his family and how he felt when doing any activities related to his hobbies. But his feelings were muddled when it came to school.

Terence esteemed some aspects of school, including some people like his favourite teacher who he considered a classic gentleman because he wore stylish old-fashioned suits and ties; and he had a vintage leather briefcase. The significant people in Terence's life were mostly adults, except for Cameron, a boy in his class. They used to spend breaks together and a true friendship formed.

## The guest

We had been working on the chapter about the unwritten rules of the classroom, when Terence decided to invite Cameron to one of our sessions. He had already learned new things about himself and wanted his friend to understand him better. He wanted my help to talk to Cameron about his autism.

Cameron accepted the invitation and we had an exciting session where he asked numerous questions and told us what he found different in Terence's ways. Cameron could not understand why Terence would eat precisely the same food every day for lunch and, if the canteen did not have sausage rolls, he would not eat anything. The two boys did not have many other friends at school. If any at all. Talking about autism seemed to have strengthened their friendship.

## The outcome

Terence continued to attend our weekly sessions for the next two years, frequently revisiting some topics from our cherished book. The chapters we used the most were: 'Feelings and emotions'; 'Teachers and asking for help'; 'The unwritten rules of the classroom'; 'Situations at school'; and 'Friends, classmates and the other children'.

My role in that school as part of the pastoral team involved being a year group tutor and personal coach. I had weekly coaching sessions with all learners in my group. It therefore made sense to merge the autism awareness sessions with coaching to avoid Terence having two sessions per week. I had devised the Relate model (presented in the next chapter) and used it in the coaching sessions, so I blended Relate with the activities from the book about Asperger's, when working with Terence. Gradually, the combination of coaching and conversations about autism became my strategy to support other young people on the spectrum and, in turn, this developed into the 'Tangram Method'.

**The Tangram Method**

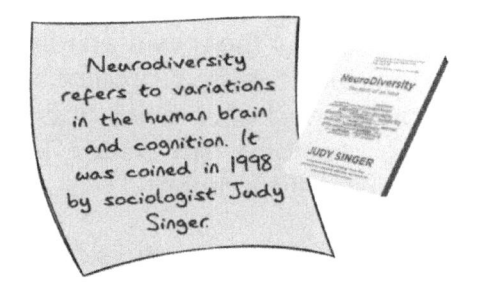

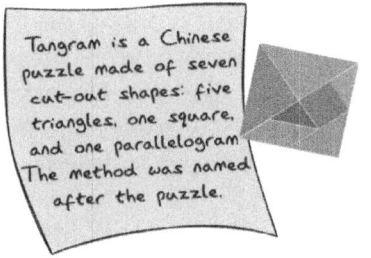

*Figure 1: The birth of the concept of Neurodiversity (Singer, 2017)*

*Figure 2: What's tangram?*

## Albert

*he/him/his*

Albert was a delightful young man with a deep voice and posh accent. Albert was polite and well mannered, however, he often missed the subtle body language of his interlocutors and carried on speaking endlessly.

Albert spoke profusely about the universe and its galaxies in his complex language, sometimes reciting some well-known quote or scientific expression. It took me some time to start seeing Albert's insecurities through his well-built masking behaviours (Goffman, 1959) that mirrored that of a scientist in the making.

Albert often found himself frustrated when he couldn't endure the entirety of a lesson, even if it happened to be one of his favourite subjects. In a peculiar turn of events on one occasion, Albert chose to position himself beneath a table with the intention of evading social interactions; ironically, this choice only intensified the attention he received. On different occasions, Albert would simply withdraw from a situation when he found it challenging to process the events and respond appropriately.

One day, after sitting in a corridor with his head down by his knees for some time, Albert lifted his head, looked at me and said,

> 'Well, that was rough!'

I asked what had been rough and he said,

> 'My brain just froze. That was rough!'

That sentence marked the beginning of a new phase, as, from that day forward, we opened up a new channel of communication.

## The beginning

When Albert had a shutdown, he would sit in the usual position, in the same spot in the corridor. I would stay nearby, until Albert would speak to me with some form of assessment like 'this was a long one' or 'that was quick!'. However, sometimes the shutdown would last longer and I had to leave for a few moments. Some staff, seeing him in that position and assuming he was alone and distressed, would check how he was. That well-meaning attempt to interact with him during a shutdown would, in turn, trigger his brain again, restarting the whole process – sometimes with the addition of a repetitive verbal pattern, like continuously reciting the digits of pi or repeatedly saying 'I don't know' in response to anything said to him.

## The card

After this resetting by other people had happened a few times, I realised we needed a way to stop other people from trying to communicate with Albert when he had a shutdown. I started leaving a communication card, with the disclaimer next to Albert: 'Please, don't speak with me. I'll be fine soon'. I would then tell him the card was there, reassuring him that people could read it and leave him in peace. I always used the exact same words, 'Your card is there, no one will disturb you'.

## The Tangram Method

Subsequently, the dynamics evolved to the next stage. After Albert sat in the corridor, I would do the card routine and leave. Staff felt freed from the obligation to check on him; and the knowledge that no one would press his reset button gave him reassurance. I had an agreement with Albert that he would bring the card back to me once the shutdown was over. Albert followed that rule religiously; and we noticed his shutdowns gradually became short lived.

When returning the card, Albert followed a routine, he would stand near my desk looking refreshed, hand the card to me and add a little comment about how the shutdown went, with some sense of celebration when each episode seemed shorter than the previous one. We both celebrated the strategy working.

Unlike Terence years earlier, Albert did not enjoy weekly sessions and did not feel he needed something regular. Albert valued the moments of reflection after an incident. That was how he seemed to learn better about his autistic traits and how to manage expectations, including his own. We would always sit together and reflect after each shutdown episode; then, we called these conversations our 'autism awareness sessions'. We would reflect on what had happened immediately before the shutdown in an attempt to identify the precise moment when Albert realised that he had to walk away and sit in the corridor.

By reflecting, Albert learned about his triggers and reactions. In turn, he found a new strategy, walking out of the classroom to the familiar corridor and doing laps around the building instead of sitting down. Albert called this his 'pacing mode'. The pacing mode helped prevent the shutdown mode; and he felt it was more socially acceptable, therefore, less anxiety-inducing. Most people seeing him walking around would probably assume he was simply going from place A to B. You probably know that some autistic children stim; a well-known stimming movement is rocking back and forth. But stimming presents itself in different ways. For Albert, it was pacing. I realised Albert was much happier knowing that the pacing gave him some control over the shutdowns, which used to upset him. Because we wanted to understand this better, we agreed to have a longer and more structured session to further explore the shutdowns.

## The extended session

That day, we both learned immensely from Albert's efforts to translate his cognitive processes into a language I could understand. I used nearly the entire block of Post-it notes, writing down single words, phrases, expressions and complete sentences to capture Albert's insights. The paper squares seemed to multiply rapidly, forming a complex mind map.

That was our most prolonged and profound autism awareness session; it produced an incredible moment of clarity for Albert. He had figured out how disempowering his acceptance of the shutdowns as inevitable had been, as the pacing strategy had revealed the cycle could be broken. It was the first time Albert had looked that deep into his emotional reaction to events. Albert preferred rational analyses and mathematical paradigms as opposed to matters of subjectivity. But that day was different.

All the emotions seemed to have a logical explanation; even the things he considered irrational in his behaviour (like hiding in plain sight under a table) made sense when analysed in context. It was a breakthrough. If this was athletic training, Albert had achieved a personal best that day. I had to do something with those Post-it notes to take stock of all the emerging knowledge from Albert's experience. With Albert's assistance, I produced a summary to share with colleagues who worked with Albert.

## The summary presented to colleagues

Albert and I discussed how some autistic traits affected his daily life and examined the shutdowns in detail; this is where his autism has a significant impact on his learning.

**The Tangram Method**

We discussed the factors that can trigger the shutdown, as well as what the shutdown mode is, how it presents itself to other people and how Albert experiences it. We focused on a significant aspect of it, the verbal loop that we named pseudo-dialogue to indicate that this is not a true two-way interaction. The following is a summary of what we learned.

*The stages leading to a shutdown*

*Stage 1: The triggers*

Triggers can be situations that create cognitive or emotional pressure and cause a reaction. Albert identified some of these triggers such as: changes in routine; a new topic unexpectedly introduced; a concept that Albert finds hard to grasp; or a different way of solving a mathematical algorithm compared to one with which Albert is familiar. He perceives these occurrences as causing stress, anxiety, the need for escapism and the need for a defence mechanism. Albert's triggers are predominantly of a cognitive nature, with only a small minority relating to social anxieties.

*Stage 2: The shutdown and pseudo-dialogue*

Once triggered, Albert may start a shutdown silently or accompanied by some verbal stimming. Occasionally, silence and verbal stimming appear intermittently in the same crisis, depending on the occurrence of new triggers. For Albert, the shutdown mode is a state of mind that manifests physically, as he must sit or lie down on the floor, motionless, silent and not listening to anyone's voice. Alternatively, he will walk continuously for some time at a certain pace. The surrounding noises usually do not influence him, but human interaction will. Therefore, Albert needs processing time alone.

The pseudo-dialogue is a strategy to block interactions by disallowing input. It consists of continuously repeating a sentence or a response pattern, even when different questions are asked. He may answer, for instance, 'Why am I like this?' to any question. Showing that Albert most likely did not process the actual question, the default answer is disconnected from the interaction and is part of his internal dialogue while searching for a resolution.

When trying to understand what happens on these occasions, from a cognitive perspective, Albert reflected on if he realises he is repeating words or sentences; and if he could stop doing that if he wanted to do so. He concluded that during these moments, although he is aware that his brain is stuck in the verbal repetition, he is not sure if he can control it. He thinks he needs to continue until it fades away. Albert described his shutdowns as a wave of darkness that stops his brain from functioning properly and causing him utter frustration with himself.

*Stage 3: The resolution*

When the dark wave is gone and the cognitive abilities return, the resolution is reached. Albert always verbalises his sense of relief when that stage is reached. Resolution does not come easily and Albert recognises he needs some reassurance when transitioning towards the final moments of the shutdown, when the communication channels gradually reopen. Albert would like to come back to discuss this transition process in the future.

### Cognitive flow

Once we understood the mechanics of the process of switching from normal mental functioning to the shutdown situation and back to functioning, we devised a flowchart to illustrate how information navigates Albert's cognition during a shutdown episode. That flowchart is presented here in the following diagram.

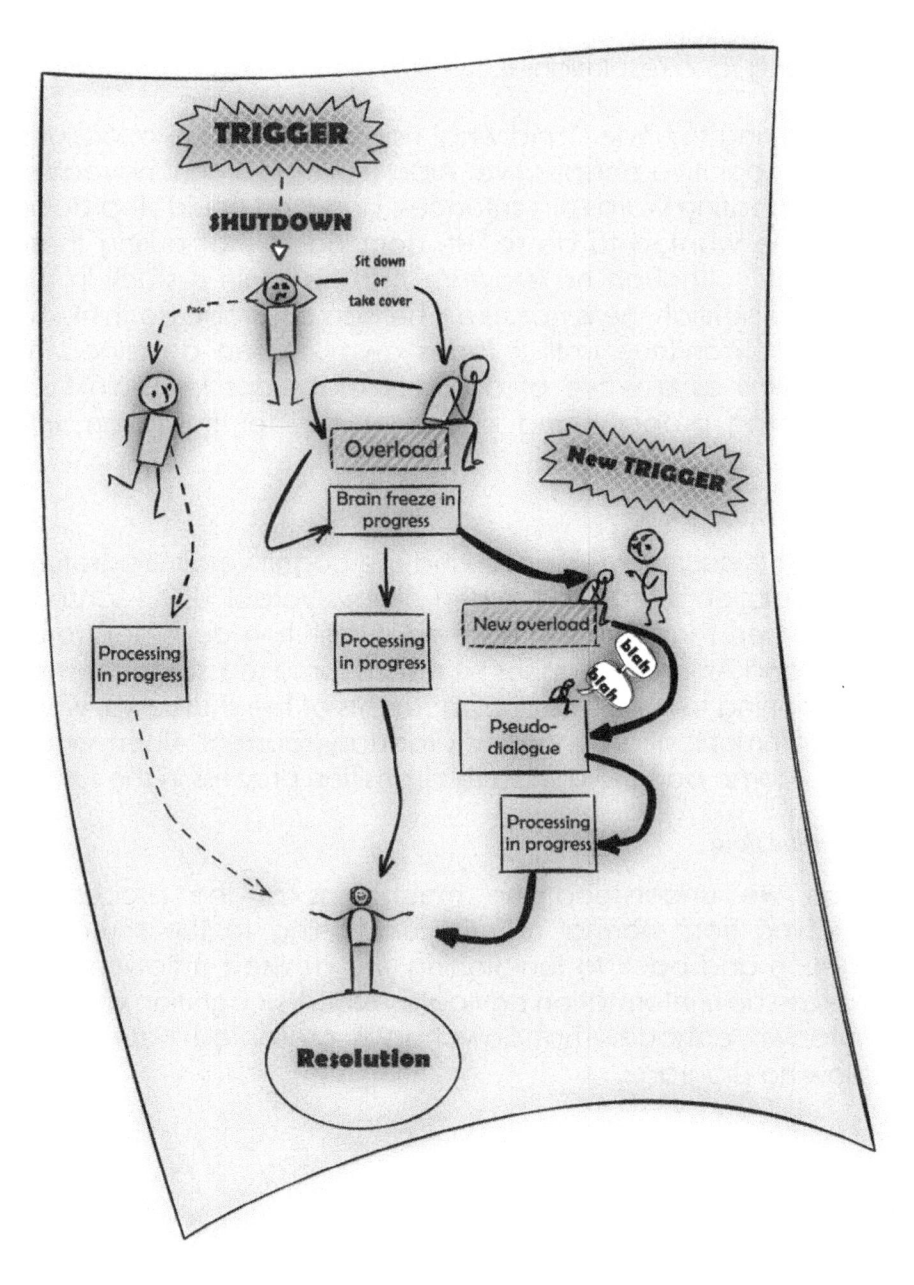

*Figure 3: Albert's cognitive flow according to himself.*

## The outcome

Albert had a positive year working with a bespoke timetable, with most subjects being taught individually. It was part of a planned transitional period that allowed Albert to continue his education, fill in any gaps in knowledge caused by occasional absences from lessons, and build up his ability to return to the mainstream classroom the following year.

The outcome of this transition intervention was gratifying to all involved, as Albert started the new year in a new group that had not witnessed any shutdowns, permitting a fresh start.

The following year, Albert attended all lessons with his year group; made effective use of a note-taker; kept up with the pace of the class without the interference of shutdowns; and undertook the tests with his peers. This allowed teachers to continuously assess his progress and provide feedback and guidance.

Like many things that year, this success story was interrupted by a global pandemic. Similar to many young people around the world, Albert found it challenging to return to the classroom after the long lockdown, worsened by contradicting guidance on the use of face coverings and distinct regulations for schools in contrast to those for the rest of the population.

Like many other neurodivergent young people, Albert struggled with the constant changes and regular lesson cancellations due to rules around Covid-19 and self-isolation.

After months dealing with much uncertainty and its side effects, Albert was transferred to a distance learning programme to permit him the academic progress he wanted. Fortunately, Albert moved on after achieving great self-awareness and a genuine sense of ownership of his learning.

## Nicole

*she/her/hers*

When I first met Nicole, she was looking for a book about ADHD as she was told I had a collection of pocketbooks about different learning difficulties.

Nicole was interested in the volume about ADHD because that was her diagnosis. Nicole borrowed that volume for a few days. She found the book interesting. However, she did not identify with the explanations of the pocketbook; the only areas of difficulty she identified with were some sensory issues. Everything else she found unrelated. Nicole told me about a regular mental fog when she would be tired of interacting with people. Occasionally it was the noise around her, other times the flickering lights; and more often a combination of factors.

During those occasions, she would feel exhausted to the extent that she needed to sleep for hours in the middle of the day. Nicole was an enthusiastic writer. However, she found learning in a big classroom extremely exhausting because of its social aspects, which affected her writing ability. After speaking at length about what seemed to me sensory overload, Nicole borrowed another book from my collection, the volume about autism.

## The beginning

A few weeks later, when Nicole returned the book, before saying any greetings, she declared,

'This book is all about me', followed by a deep sigh that I was unsure if it meant relief or grief.

She identified with most areas of difficulties mentioned in the little book, such as: social communication; social interactions; social imagination; sensory difficulties; a love of routine; and aversion to change.

She felt confused because she had believed for a long time that the reason for her difficulties was ADHD, but now she had a different theory. We talked about how some of these conditions overlap and how sometimes the diagnosis depends on which professional carried out the assessment.

Despite being somewhat confused, Nicole was glad to finally understand why she felt overwhelmed with sounds, lights and interaction with people. It gave her a sense of normality because reading those things described in a book meant it was real and other people felt the same.

Nicole asked to keep the book for a few more days because she wanted to take notes and think more about everything. She finally returned the book and we talked again about autism. Nicole seemed to enjoy talking about her reflections and telling me how she felt on particular days, such as after a lesson in which everyone seemed to be talking simultaneously and the whole experience was so exhausting she had to nap afterwards.

## The elusive words

On many occasions, Nicole wanted to discuss how she tried to understand what was happening in her brain when she could not articulate any words. On those occasions, she felt frustrated because the words would simply not come out of her mouth, even if they were stuck in her brain in a complex puzzle. Nicole had a passion for words, so being unable to process her thoughts to turn them into words was unbelievably frustrating. Those moments made Nicole doubt herself and her ability to become a writer if she could not use words proficiently.

We decided to have a regular meeting and agreed that Nicole would bring something she had thought about over the week, questions she wanted to ask, and things she had found out and wanted to share. It was the beginning of our autism awareness sessions.

Nicole came to see me most weeks, sometimes bringing new questions and occasionally telling me of her discoveries. In one of those weeks, she told me she had realised she would like to have an assessment and potentially a formal diagnosis.

## The Ryuu card game

In the meantime, Nicole continued to attend our sessions with some regularity, but they never became rigidly structured or formal. They mostly happened outside because Nicole found it easier to think when outdoors. Our focus remained on Nicole's needs on that particular day. However, I wanted to introduce some structure to the sessions. I had acquired a set of play cards designed around autistic traits and had not tried them yet.

So, in one of our unplanned sessions, I took those cards out and asked Nicole if she would like to look at them with me. Ryuu is a non-competitive game of dragons aimed at teaching social skills (Shaul, 2009).

Nicole was not interested in the symbology of dragons and could not relate them to autism. So, for our sessions, I focused on using the dragon's descriptors and evolution processes to pinpoint autistic traits which with she identified. Based on that, we selected the cards that represented Nicole and discarded all the others. We then had a deck of cards that covered most of Nicole's ways of thinking; she was pleased with that and expressed a sense of relief to finally explain who she was in a way that could make sense. We revisited Nicole's deck several times over the months, when she mentioned things that happened to her and she recognised something from the Ryuu descriptions. She loved sharing those moments. Nicole's main wish was to make sense of herself and have a sense of identity that felt acceptable to herself.

## The outcome

After a lengthy assessment process, Nicole's parents received her diagnosis, confirming what she already knew, she was autistic. We continued our sessions, occasionally over a few months, until Nicole finished school. She now knew she could wear noise-cancelling headphones, shaded glasses to reduce light input, and take regular breaks from sensory input. She knew the power of having a walk outdoors, letting the fresh air recharge her brain. She also knew she could take time off from writing when the words did not flow – without panicking or falling into the self-doubt trap. She was going to be the writer she wanted to be, only a fully self-aware and proud neurodivergent one.

## Georgie

*she/her/hers*

Georgie had a strong interest in science and a passion for animal welfare. Georgie's records indicated she was autistic. However, most people would not notice any significant differences in her behaviour compared with her peers, until very recently, when she had become unusually quiet and occasionally would not provide a verbal answer when asked a question.

I was pleased when Georgie came to see me. When she entered my office, I said the usual almost automatic:

'Can I help you?' to which she replied with a touch of annoyance,

'Well, I was told you were the person to ask for help if I needed, so I assume you can.'

I immediately appreciated Georgie's directness and honesty. I was familiar with that mindset and liked it a lot. Despite the weight of the responsibility of such a statement, I was happy to try.

Georgie explained that she was autistic and always managed things well, but lately some things were not feeling right. She was not aware why, but she was never good at explaining her thoughts and feelings anyway, she added.

## The beginning

Georgie had no qualms identifying as autistic and had no reservations with the language of it. She even enjoyed the fact that once people knew she was autistic they would usually leave her alone assuming she did not want to socialise, which was often true. However, her anxieties had grown so fast lately that she lost track of what made her anxious in the first place and had no idea how to tame it.

At that point, Georgie felt she could not cope by herself anymore; and she hated the idea of bothering people, having to find out when would be convenient to speak with someone. If I had some advice, she would gladly try it, as long as it made sense, she cautiously added. We agreed on which times would work for both of us to meet regularly, that way she would not need to guess when to ask for help or when it would be convenient for me, as this was one of her main concerns.

## The animals

Georgie came for a chat at our pre-agreed time on a few occasions after that day. She always spoke lengthily about loving animals and how she felt the mutual understanding she had with them, which she found far more complicated to develop with humans. She was bothered by people using 'in-between-the-lines' meanings, metaphors and, worst of all, telling socially accepted lies, which Georgie believed made true communication simply impossible. She did not like it when people told lies and called it kindness or diplomacy, because lies are lies.

Georgie believed that most people lied frequently, for that reason she could never trust anyone because she could not distinguish a lie from the truth. Animals do not lie, she said with conviction and pride. According to Georgie, her animals always knew if she was feeling down and they also knew how to cheer her up. Most people would feel lost and pressured to help, talking too much, patronising at times, suggesting obviously unhelpful solutions or simply being too close when all she needed was to be left alone for a while.

Georgie struggled with social situations, because people do odd things, behave randomly and say one thing and mean something else – then expect you to know what they mean. She wished people were straightforward, spoke the truth without worrying about hurting each other's feelings all the time (or getting hurt by the truth) and could be authentic friends. Like her animals. If you don't like my hairstyle, you can tell me and it will not hurt me because it is only your opinion, she argued.

Despite always knowing of her diagnosis, what Georgie had learned about the autism spectrum at this point was the aspects commonly known but not specific to her own traits. Despite being aware that each autistic person was different, she was interested in understanding it better and deepening her self-awareness. I suggested the Ryuu card game as a resource to support our conversations around autism, because Nicole had found it helpful. Georgie was happy to give the cards a go.

**The play cards are back**

I followed the same approach I had used before with Nicole. Georgie read the description of each dragon and decided if a card was going in her pile or to be discarded. Once Georgie finished separating the cards, I named the chosen pile

## The Tangram Method

'Georgie's recipe' and removed the discarded cards. It was the first time that the notion of a unique recipe emerged.

It seemed a simple way to explain the many recognised autistic traits and the notion that each autistic person only presents a certain number of them. Also, not only does each person have only some traits, but they also form a unique individual combination. Therefore, each person has their totally unique recipe, which comprises specific traits in a distinctive combination, alongside other individual characteristics such as personality and life experiences.

This idea of a unique recipe made sense to Georgie, as she had autistic friends with whom she got along well but who were also completely different from her and from each other. She used to say, we are a very unusual bunch of individualities, all equally autistic, but likewise autistic in different ways. They were just equally differently autistic!

'Oh, that is why you speak of neurodiversity,' she exclaimed. 'I see it now!' she stated in a mixture of relief and achievement.

Georgie came to see me most weeks and we always used the Ryuu cards to support our conversations. She liked picking up her chosen cards, flicking through them and selecting the dragons that had been more noticeable to her that week. She seemed to find it calming to have time within her busy week to stop and reflect. Georgie did not consider herself a reflective person, except when she was in our sessions. Outside our conversations, she often avoided overthinking, as her thoughts tended to circle endlessly around various aspects of her life. When she was in our conversations, she knew I would ask her a question or two. This was enough to help her busy brain focus on one aspect at a time to reflect and talk about that.

## The outcome

In her final session, Georgie brought me a lovely card saying our sessions had taught her the importance of accepting that we are all very different; that sometimes humans can also be good company and even friends, despite most not being as trustworthy as animals.

## Rowan

*they/them/theirs*

Rowan had some friends who had a diagnosis of autism and these friends' explanations of what made them autistic were all too familiar to Rowan, especially how they found it hard to communicate and interact with people.

Rowan felt there were so many similarities that they considered the possibility of being autistic as well. Rowan researched about autism and the more they learned about it, the more convinced they were of being autistic. That was why they had come to see me, to ask if doing these autism awareness sessions would help them to find out if they were autistic.

I told them that for a diagnosis they would need to see a specific type of professional and signposted them to different routes to get an assessment should they want it. I explained that the awareness sessions were systematic conversations, focused on what the young person wanted to reflect and, because of their open-ended format, I would be willing to adapt them to their goals.

## The beginning

Rowan decided to try a couple of sessions to see if talking would help them make some sense of what they had in their head. They would then decide if it was worth the effort of pursuing a diagnosis, as Rowan was aware there was a long waiting list. Rowan was the first young person I had started the autism awareness sessions with who had no official diagnosis.

I found it challenging to start with, as it was a new experience and I was not certain this would work. I did not want to assume that Rowan was autistic nor confirm or refute their self-diagnosis, as this was not my role here. For that reason, my only choice was to listen and try to ask relevant non-leading questions to help them come to their own conclusions.

## The neurodiversity cards

Before Rowan had come to see me, I had received the prototype of the cards I was developing to replace the Ryuu game. Because Rowan was unsure for how long they would want to meet and I was uncertain how the sessions would turn out given the various unknowns, I thought using the new cards could be a way to grasp Rowan's goals while having something tangible to work with.

I explained to Rowan that using the cards would be an excellent opportunity for me to trial them; at the same time, the activity would give us a starting point. Rowan was keen to try the cards and, in turn played a decisive role in identifying design issues and other details only someone with that level of attention to detail would notice. The outcomes indicated that it was a fitting strategy to combine reviewing the card game with the exploratory nature of our agreed sessions.

When using the neurodiversity cards with Rowan, I followed the same procedure I had done with the Ryuu game. I asked Rowan to select the cards based on affinity, piling up to the left the ones that resonated with them and to the right the ones that did not. Rowan created a third pile in the middle with the cards they were unsure if they should go left or right.

I took a photo of the selection of cards to keep a record of the choices, because I realised we would probably want to revisit the activity later to make a decision about the uncertain pile. I suggested we excluded only the cards Rowan definitely did not identify with and kept both the chosen and the undecided ones together for the moment. We agreed to rethink the card selection later to finalise Rowan's recipe.

Throughout that first session, it was informative to observe Rowan's individuality in the way they positioned and perfectly aligned and balanced the cards on the table – meticulously following a rigorous order and layout, painstakingly ensuring the display looked symmetrical, perfectly aligned and balanced. Rowan continued to be meticulous with the card display anytime we worked with them again. We talked about colour combinations and how colours relate to each other because Rowan had a particular interest in colour theory and provided constructive feedback about my colour choices for the cards.

In preparation for our next session, Rowan completed an online autism quotient test (Baron-Cohen, 2001). We had spoken about the use of the test as non-clinical screening, which would give Rowan merely an indication of autistic traits, not a diagnosis. In the session, we discussed Rowan's answers. They talked me through their answers one by one, explaining how they had reached a decision on each choice.

Listening to Rowan's explanations and reasoning behind the choices, I realised they had researched autism for quite some time and had developed a solid understanding of the condition, having a vast vocabulary. Rowan's self-awareness was remarkable, as they seemed to have dedicated time and effort to reflect and try out strategies in different situations. Rowan held a rigid opinion on certain topics – taking the classic black or white approach – and Rowan was fully aware of that. They were confident that this was a more reliable approach to most things in life; they did not like the idea of grey areas, they told me.

## The personality typology

Even though Rowan seemed convinced they were autistic and was seeking some validation, my role was not to endorse or contest their viewpoints. I realised we needed to look at other factors that could help Rowan in their self-discovery process. Having studied Jung typology in my early career (Jung, 2017), I decided to introduce a check on personality type.

I wanted to find out Rowan's type to discuss with them if the combination of personality and self-identified autistic traits made sense to them. I described the personality typology in simple terms and directed Rowan to two of the tests which use Jung typology and the Myers Briggs available online; then I asked them to choose one to complete before our next meeting.

## Rowan's personality type

Rowan's type was ISTJ which means: **introverted, sensing, thinking** and **judging**. When reading the descriptions of personal characteristics for ISTJs, such as the learning styles and communication preferences, Rowan found they resonated with their self-image. As a matter of fact, the ISTJ type has many commonalities with a generic description of an autistic person.

Therefore, Rowan found many correlations between the autistic traits with which they identify and the ISTJ type, particularly introversion and thinking. After my experience with Rowan, I was convinced that combining the personality type and the trait recipe can reveal insights into aspects of the young person's behaviours, their ways of thinking and communicating with others. Similarly, Rowan found the activity insightful.

## The outcome

After a full cycle of sessions, Rowan concluded they would request an autism assessment, as they were more convinced than ever of being autistic and felt that a diagnosis would give the validation they needed. Rowan had achieved their goal with the autism awareness sessions and now had personal plans in mind when we finished the programme.

## Ace

*he/him/his*

Ace's mother called to explain that Ace was autistic and did not want any additional help with his learning. He would appreciate it if no one spoke to him about being autistic, as he found the topic unnecessary and unhelpful.

A few weeks later, Ace's mother called again to say he told her a substitute teacher had told students 'to do some stupid task' and he would never go back to school. His mother was worried because she knew Ace was capable of keeping that promise. Fortunately, after some rationalisation over the events of that day, Ace agreed to come to see me and he went back to his classroom the next day.

## The beginning

After that first conversation, it became customary for Ace's mother to call me when Ace came home frustrated about something. Those occasions gave me opportunities to develop a positive rapport with him. Ace started to come to ask about something he was unsure about or to tell me something had annoyed him, like the second time a substitute teacher told him to do what he considered 'a stupid task'.

For the first time, Ace mentioned autism as a factor and added casually that he knew little about it. I told him about the autism awareness sessions I had done, in case he would be interested. The next time I saw Ace was when he came to ask if we could have those autism awareness sessions I spoke about.

When we started having weekly sessions, I noticed he was already well versed in his autism; his main motivation for coming to these meetings was to improve his interactions with other people. However, he assured me he did not like people and did not care about their views on him either.

Ace had strong views on social protocols and was comfortable in his own ways. But he was aware that other people had different views and expected him to be more sociable, so he wanted to comprehend the neurotypical mindset associated with commonly accepted behaviours, such as diplomatic lies.

Gaining insight into the complexities of neurotypical behaviour aided Ace in embracing the diversity of individuals. It reinforced the notion that differences exist without a definitive right or wrong, as long as we can coexist harmoniously without imposing or expecting conformity from one another.

The conventional social rules create expectations that usually are not in tune with the autistic mind. For some children and young people, this creates a sense of inability to meet expectations. This mismatch is commonly a result of the double empathy problem, because often adults fail to appreciate how a neurodivergent mind operates and, consequently, also fail to help them appreciate how the neurotypical world works.

## The outcome

After completing a full autism awareness programme, Ace expressed his perceptions of how these sessions had been helpful in raising his self-awareness and broadening his understanding of his autism, especially in contrast to his neurotypical counterparts and incredibly dissimilar fellow neurodivergent relatives. On several occasions, he provided positive feedback about how these discussions helped in his self-esteem and a potentially better wellbeing throughout his life.

## Max

*he/him/they/them*

Max had finished school and was already working part time. He had received his autism report and wanted to know 'what to do with it'. The diagnosis was not a surprise, but the emptiness that followed was.

'I am autistic, so what do I do with that piece of information?'

Max felt underwhelmed with their diagnosis because the recommendations 'specific to child' (sic) in the report were too generic. The report was thought-provoking because it provided a comprehensive timeline of Max's development from birth, through the primary school years and up to the time of the assessment.

However, the diagnosis had arrived at a time when Max was set to have the most significant step of his young life so far: going to university. Looking forward, as opposed to dwelling on what had happened, was a must at this point.

Conversely, the report was naturally written in retrospection; therefore, it did not offer enough clues on how being autistic would affect future stages of life, such as the imminent change. His chosen university was in a different city and the plan was to live in student accommodation, get a new part-time job and be a fully grown independent adult. Max had a few months to prepare for all that and was fully aware that change was not his strong suit; he did not feel confident in dealing with unpredictability, either.

We agreed to learn about his autism together, identify his traits, and understand how they may help with the preparation for the big move. We also wanted to identify areas he might need to work on harder to overcome barriers.

## The beginning

To help me to know Max better, I asked him to complete the autism quotient questionnaire. In the next session we discussed his answers one by one, trying to analyse the motivation behind each choice. Using the same approach I had used with Rowan and Ace, I colour-coded the answers based on how high each would score on the autism scale.

Although this is an overly simplistic way of looking at the matter, this activity enables the young person to visualise their individual spectrum of traits and also permits me to comprehend them better. However, Max's answers seemed to cover a wide range of the spectrum, suggesting he presented the vast majority of the traits used in that questionnaire.

Furthermore, in each question, Max had chosen the answer with the highest score on the autism quotient scale. However, Max's outlook did not seem to confirm such a high score as he did not present classic autistic behaviours, so that high score intrigued me and rang loud alarm bells on my marking detector.

## The interests

Max's interests revolved around art, creativity, philosophy and social justice matters, which was a contrasting combination to the young people I had done autism awareness sessions with up to that point.

Max was articulate and proficient, always verbalising his ideas with remarkable clarity, critical thinking and logic. He had a small group of friends with whom he attended social events quite often. He presented a high level of autonomy and original thinking, but also seemed to be impacted by external expectations while fully aware of his natural preferences, which would often oppose those expectations.

Max had developed a highly sophisticated camouflaging behaviour that steered people into thinking he was neurotypical. His ways to negotiate those contradictions and sustain a presentation that was true to himself, but also responded to what he knew was expected of him, was astonishing to the observer and unequivocally exhausting to him.

Following from the positive outcome of using the personality typology with Rowan and Ace previously, I asked Max to take a test and then discuss the result in our next session. Similar to Rowan, Max was also ISTJ.

Max considered the result descriptions highly accurate and useful. We had reached the final stage of our autism awareness sessions; and he needed to make the final preparations before moving to the other city. We used the neurodiversity cards to identify and reflect about situations Max could face and drafted a rudimentary action plan on how to deal with each one. Below is the situational analysis that Max completed.

Helpful situations I identify with:

- I may not control the noises around me, so I use protection, like noise-cancelling headphones.
- I avoid noisy places, but if I cannot avoid them and cannot use headphones, I make sure to have enough quiet time afterwards to unload.
- I know people use figurative language all the time, so I have learned to make notes when I learn a new expression, so I will recognise it next time.
- I try to let people know when I need more time to answer questions, so I usually say something like, 'Can I get back to you with an answer later?'.

## The Tangram Method

Unhelpful situations I identify with that I cannot avoid but have some control over:

- I do not always know how to answer questions about myself or to give quick responses to decisions I need to make on the spot, so I shutdown.
- I avoid trying new things because I know it will take a long time to get used to them and I find the unknown uncomfortable.
- I find it difficult to make choices as I am afraid of choosing the wrong thing, hence sometimes I avoid making choices altogether.
- I can only focus on one task at a time and find it upsetting if there are distractions such as noise or flashing lights.

Unhelpful situations I identify with that I cannot avoid and have little or no control over:

I find contradictions irritating and I tend to not trust people who contradict themselves.

- I find planning challenging, because I do not know what will happen next, so I cannot make realistic plans.
- I believe each word has a meaning and I struggle when people use sayings such as 'it's raining cats and dogs' and I have no clue what they mean.

Things I can do to minimise the immediate impact of unavoidable unhelpful situations:

- Plan what is in my control, think about possible outcomes for others, display plans on a corkboard and use my phone more effectively, so I don't forget.
- Ask people the meaning of idioms they use and their meaning in that given context.

- Use strategies to minimise the environmental triggers (e.g. taking a short break from a noisy or crowded place).
- Using strategies to ask for help if in a crisis, such as communication cards.

## The outcome

Max realised he had been masking for many years, to the extent of losing touch with his true self. But he now decided he could choose to camouflage for the benefit of unaware people if he wanted to, but would continue to work hard on unmasking. Max was determined to change from the original strenuous and emotionally costly unconscious masking to a newly found deliberate camouflaging strategy, which can be a survival skill and a way to exercise compassion for those who do not know better yet. But Max wholeheartedly believes that the more people are neurodiversity aware, the less neurodivergent people need to mask (or indeed camouflage).

With Max, I learned to distinguish masking from camouflaging. Masking is when a person performs certain learned behaviours to meet others' expectations. Masking occurs mostly at an unconscious level, often causing tiredness and some loss of the sense of identity. The masking exercise draws a significant amount of energy, causing exhaustion and often fluctuations in mood.

What we called camouflaging is the active and purposeful use of learned masking behaviours in a cautious manner. Once masking becomes conscious, it is possible to develop new habits to counteract the seemingly natural learned behaviours by unmasking. Like a smart chameleon, the neurodivergent person takes ownership of their masking when and if, they see it as situationally helpful to them or others. Camouflaging happens at the conscious level, allowing the person to take breaks, verbalise their actions and stop camouflaging at any point.

## The Tangram Method

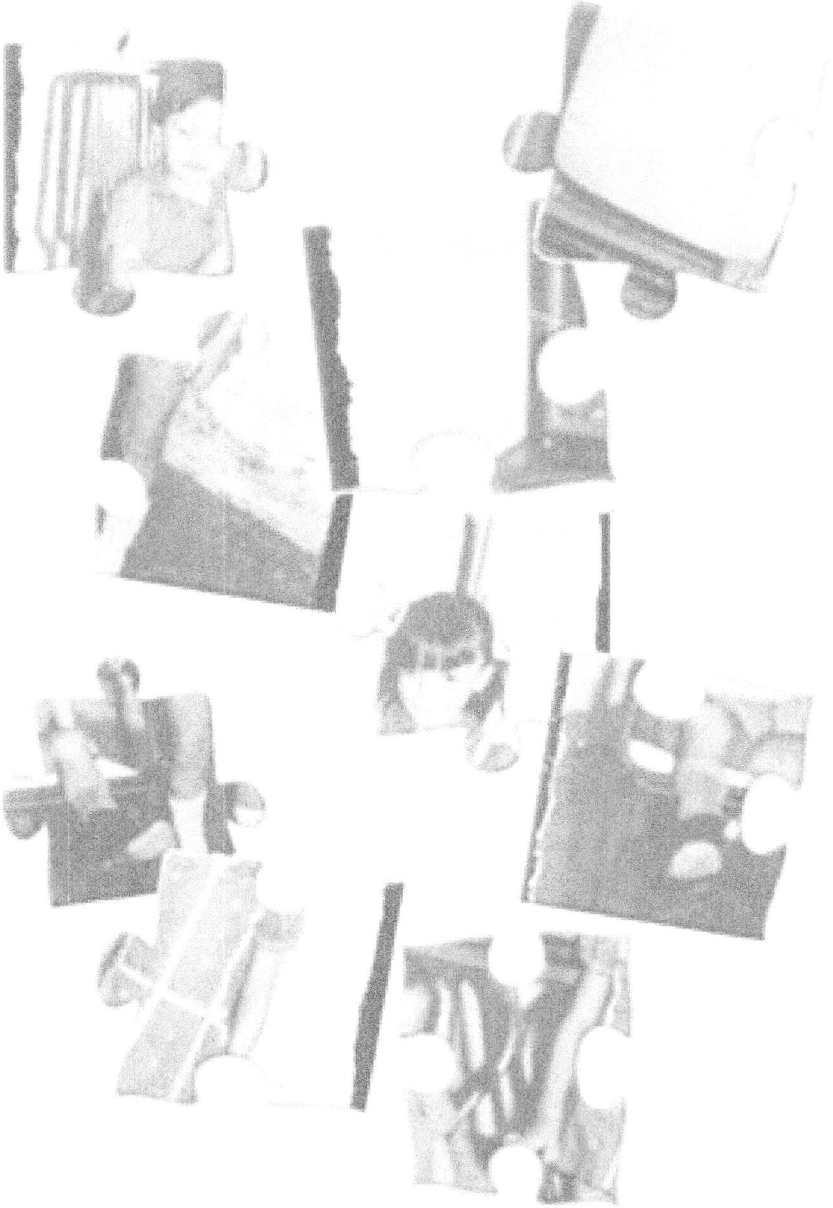

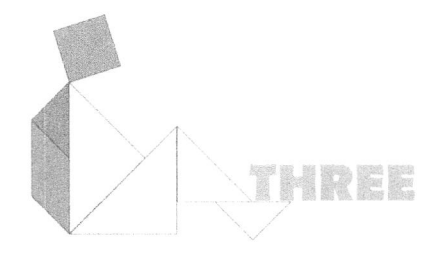

# The approach before the method

Tangram is a Chinese puzzle consisting of seven cut-out geometric shapes used to create various figures. The goal is to use all seven pieces without overlapping them. Like the jigsaw puzzle, the tangram is classified as a dissection puzzle, where pieces are cut into geometric shapes. However, the key difference between these two brainteasers lies in how the solution is achieved.

While a jigsaw puzzle has numerous pieces and only one fixed, predetermined solution, a tangram has a set number of pieces (seven) but can create a vast array of figures. For this reason, I find the tangram to be a more suitable metaphor for the autism spectrum.

Later in this book, I explain my analogy in more detail and why this is the reason I associate autism with the tangram rather than the traditional jigsaw puzzle piece. However, I would first like to offer a visual representation of my perception of these two puzzles and how I relate each to a different mindset. On one

## The Tangram Method

side is the jigsaw puzzle, likely more widely known, with its single solution, no matter how many pieces. On the other side is the ancient, but perhaps less popular, tangram, with its seven predetermined pieces and endless possibilities for solutions.

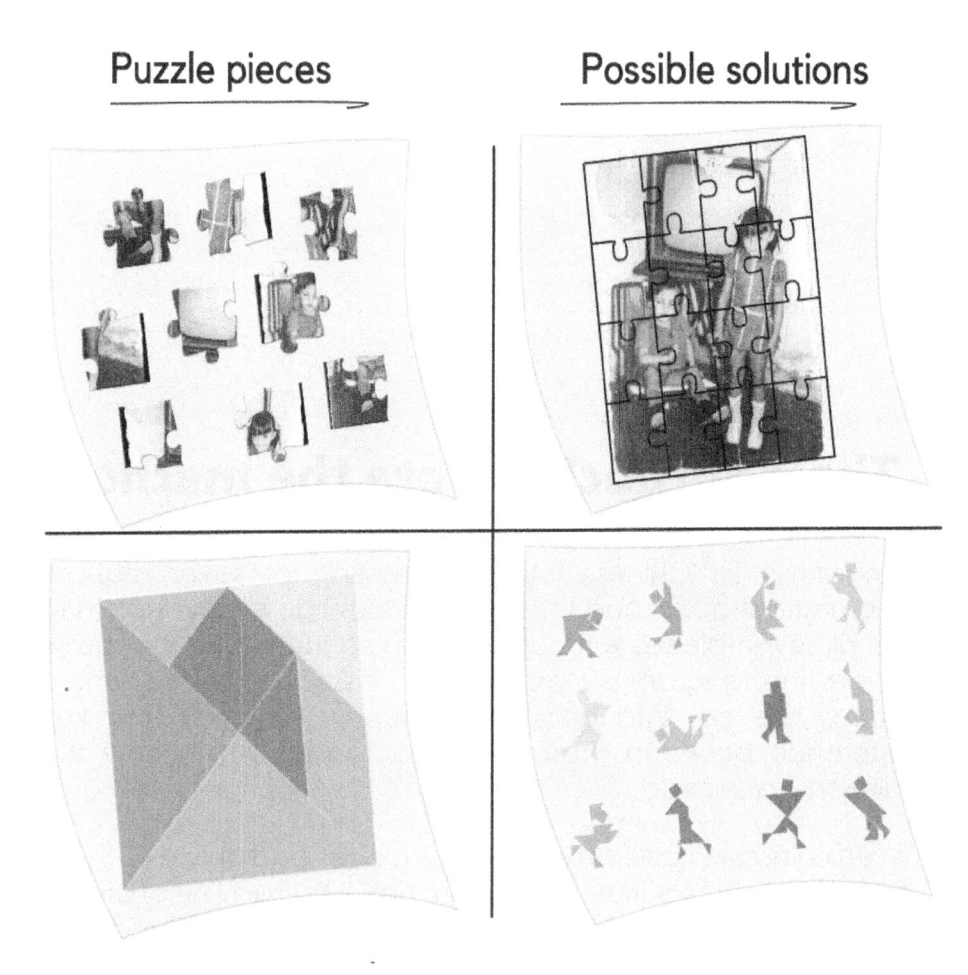

*Figure 4: Visual comparison between the jigsaw and the tangram puzzles*

The twelve figures in my illustration above are merely a demonstrative sample of the numerous possibilities. The key word here is 'possibilities' in the plural.

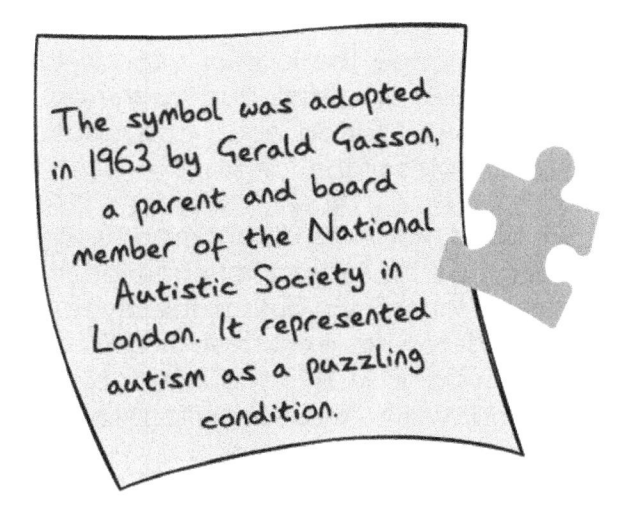

> The symbol was adopted in 1963 by Gerald Gasson, a parent and board member of the National Autistic Society in London. It represented autism as a puzzling condition.

*Figure 5: The history of the puzzle piece as symbol of autism (Gernsbacher, 2018).*

Having met many young people during my time in education, I have realised that each individual has their own unique set of cut-out shapes: their experiences, perspectives and identities. They have an infinite number of ways to combine them and express their multiple identities and roles in society.

I have always loved the tangram's ability to challenge and fascinate people of all ages. For many years, I've have kept a tangram on my desk, which often entices others to try to solve it. It has been a regular conversation starter and sometimes simply something to fidget with while quietly processing one's thoughts. The tangram on my desk has been a good friend to me and also to my friends.

Predictably, when reflecting on my approach to autism awareness conversations with young people, I realised how the principles of the tangram have influenced my thinking in more ways than one. In contrast with the close-ended jigsaw, the open-ended nature of the tangram is a better representation of this self-awareness approach.

## The Tangram Method

Resulting from the fact that I am a Freirean[1] educator who believes in the knowledge the learner already brings to the table, as well as a believer in 'dialogue' as the essence of the pedagogy of freedom, I faced each conversation with the same openness attributes of the tangram.

As a society, we have made significant progress since the time Bettelheim (1967). and similar scholars blamed the so-called 'refrigerator mother' for causing autism; the several decades of autism being considered an exclusively male condition; and the other myths systematically debunked over the years. Nonetheless, neurodiversity – more specifically autism – remains broadly misunderstood and stereotyped.

*Figure 6: Explanation of the concept of the refrigerator mother*

In the last five years, I have observed an increase in the literature about autism by actual autistic authors and researchers. The neurodiverse advocacy community has grown immensely; and the effects of this growth are starting to

---

[1] See References for information about Paulo Freire's pedagogy

## The approach before the method

be evident in society. However, there is still a long way to go. Regularly, young people come to see me who have little information about their diagnosis. Usually, their diagnostic report does not make sense to them, nor does it offer reliable answers to the questions they have been carrying since they can remember.

Many have become masters of masking. In some cases, the mask is so well glued to the face that they cannot tell anymore how their actual face looks. In addition, they have been praised for their masking skills. Masking has earned them a sense of normality and belonging to mainstream life, whether in school, family or friendship groups. Some of the best maskers became masters by training. They attended years of interventions at school aimed at developing social skills by learning to behave as everyone else, unlearning their individualities.

Well-intentioned professionals prescribed social activities led by adults to encourage them to make friends, while the non-autistic children learned most of their social skills unmediated by adults.

I believe that many of the young people who engaged in conversation with me about their autism were interested in understanding *their* autism and not autism as a general concept. Another element is becoming aware of their traits to make best use of them. They also want to know when their traits are seen as a barrier or when the way society is organised becomes a barrier for them.

Those young people who shared their stories with me, which I am sharing with you, form a small sample. Still, I consider it representative due to the similar patterns between their experiences and other young people within the educational system, especially the secondary years.

I was not conducting research per se, but my researcher hat kept cropping up, because of those patterns. Which gradually and organically took shape over the years and a method emerged.

But before outlining the Tangram Method, I need to take you back to its precursor, the Relate coaching model, which I devised when working in the pastoral team of a secondary school, which had a coaching system as part of their pedagogy.

The development of that model provided me with a structure for the meetings with the children I supported and became a significant step toward the work I later started doing with students on the autism spectrum. For that reason, I want to give you a glimpse of that model and how it correlates to the next stage of my approach and subsequently to the Tangram Method.

# The Relate model: the starting point

The central point of the coaching intervention is the learner in relation to themselves and others, concerning the personal background (past), current situation (present) and aspirations or fears (future). Similar to most methods, Relate is an acronym and consists of six steps which cover each session (Reality, Expectations, Language, Action, Thinking and Evaluation). The sessions aim to raise self-awareness of individual learning styles and study habits to understand how these may impact the learning outcomes.

### The pedagogical principles behind the model

#### The Freirean pedagogy

The libertarian pedagogy advocated by Paulo Freire has shown that the learning process always starts where the learner is. The learner does not come empty to the learning experience; the educator must take what the learner brings as the starting point. It is from the learner's reality that it is possible to build new knowledge.

Relate keeps this pedagogical principle in mind, allowing for the very first stage of the model to be **Reality**, which consists of an informal consideration of what the learner brings to that specific session on that particular day. This stage links the past to the present by guiding the learners to ask themselves the question: 'Where have I come from today and where do I stand?'

## Socio-constructivist pedagogy

The socio-constructivism proposed by Vygotsky (1962) advocates that cognitive development happens by the internalisation of language. Language mediates learning in various ways. Relate focuses on the use of language to organise and consolidate learning. For this reason, in every session, at the **Language** step, the coach encourages the learner to either verbalise, write or draw some element of the session topic.

## Existential pedagogy

Existential pedagogy (Malik, 2013) promotes the sense of self-worth and considers individual learners instead of a prescribed curriculum aimed at an idealised individual learner or group.

For this reason, I incorporated the **Evaluation** step to Relate to allow a pause to appreciate the moment, evaluate the gains and lessons learned and enjoy the experience. This final pause can transfer to many other aspects of the learning experience, encouraging learners to stop and appreciate their victories, whether big or small.

## Coaching principles

### Goal setting and the Expectations stage

Coaching first emerged from the sports world (Whitmore, 2017); therefore, most of its methods are designed for adults. Mainstream coaching methods benefit from the premise that sports people and corporate professionals have a relatively solid grasp of their aspirations, aims and dreams.

For younger adults and adolescents, the future is less clear and, consequently, their aspirations are unclear, undefined or ever-changing. This characteristic of teenagers brings a significant challenge to the application of the vast majority of coaching methods as those tend to start with the end in mind, the bigger target and the pursuit of the ideal world.

Younger learners are still negotiating parents' (or other adults') expectations, peer pressure and social media influence, as well as the doubts they may have about what they want to do with their lives. With that in mind, Relate follows the coaching principle of focusing on the goals but only later in the process. The idea of finding purpose or targets to pursue is part of a continuous construction by understanding the numerous expectations they deal with regularly.

# Coaching and the 'Thinking' stage

Fundamentally, all coaching methods are based on a series of questions and answers in a constant, thoughtful exercise. Some say that coaching can be a form of guided self-reflection, given that the coach's task is to promote self-questioning continuously. It is not an exercise of learning from someone but from oneself with the help and mediation of another. Relate sustains the coaching tradition and offers a moment of guided reflection, with the aim to develop it as a habit.

## The six stages of the approach

Most coaching methods consist of a series of steps the coach follows in a timed manner. The length of the sessions is fixed (30 minutes is a reasonable length) and the sessions follow the stages depending on the method used. Each letter represents a specific step of the session. The steps will drive the flow of the conversation and the boundaries for the topics.

The approach before the method

**Reality**
- What you bring
- Where you come from
- Here and now
- Self and others

**Expectations**
- Hopes and wishes
- Imagination
- Fears and doubts
- Anxieties

**Language**
- Say it
- Write it down
- Draw it
- Picture it

**Action**
- Collaborate
- Take part
- Engage
- Enterprise

**Evaluation**
- Look back, look forward
- Take in and enjoy
- Embrace
- Envisage, imagine and dream

**Thinking**
- Pause
- Self-reflection
- Conversation with others
- Hindsight

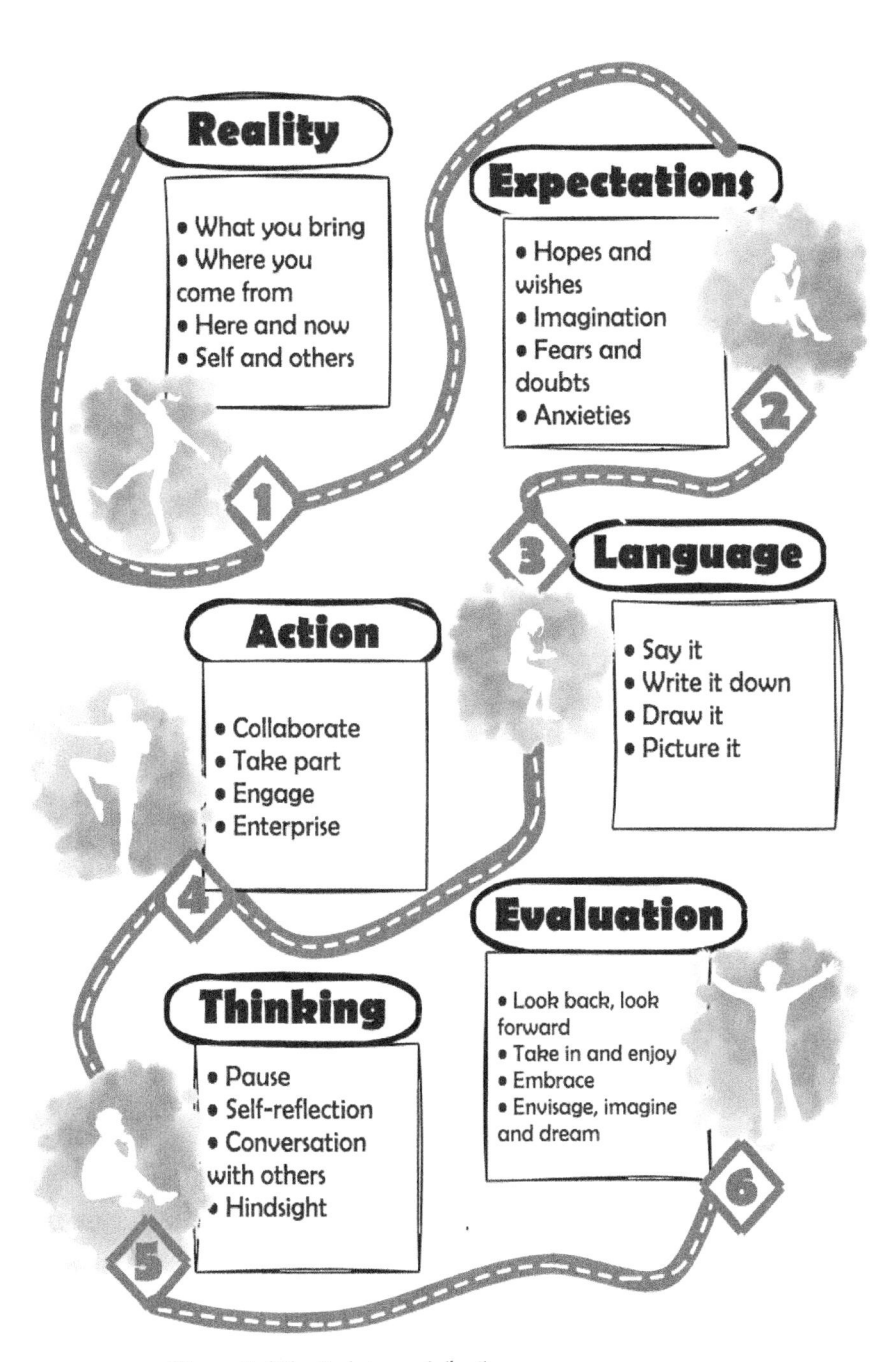

*Figure 7: The Relate model's flow*

**The Tangram Method**

### Reality

It is the here and now, the situational reality, the starting point where we all are. In that sense, the opening of each session is always about the here and now.

### Expectations

This step includes individual expectations and those of the significant others. This includes the positive and negative feelings about the near future.

### Language

This is the dialogue itself. The third step in any session would encourage some level of expressing thoughts in the form of language.

## Action

This step must include a practical activity. At this point, the young person is asked to complete a form or questionnaire, draw a picture or go around searching for a specific object.

## Thinking

The Thinking step is a moment for reflection, to consider what they have done today and record it in a learning log. They can simply be quiet for a while to think with a focus in mind.

## Evaluation

This is time to reflect and assess. The aim is to develop the habit of evaluating what worked well and what did not. It is an opportunity to enjoy the moment and also rate the usefulness of the session.

## The Tangram Method

One critical element of most coaching practices is that the individual being coached needs to engage with the programme voluntarily. For that reason, Relate is not meant as a prescribed intervention. The young person needs to be fully informed about the possible benefits and the limitations of the programme to make a decision about engaging or not. To help manage expectations, an informed consent form is completed prior to starting the individual sessions.

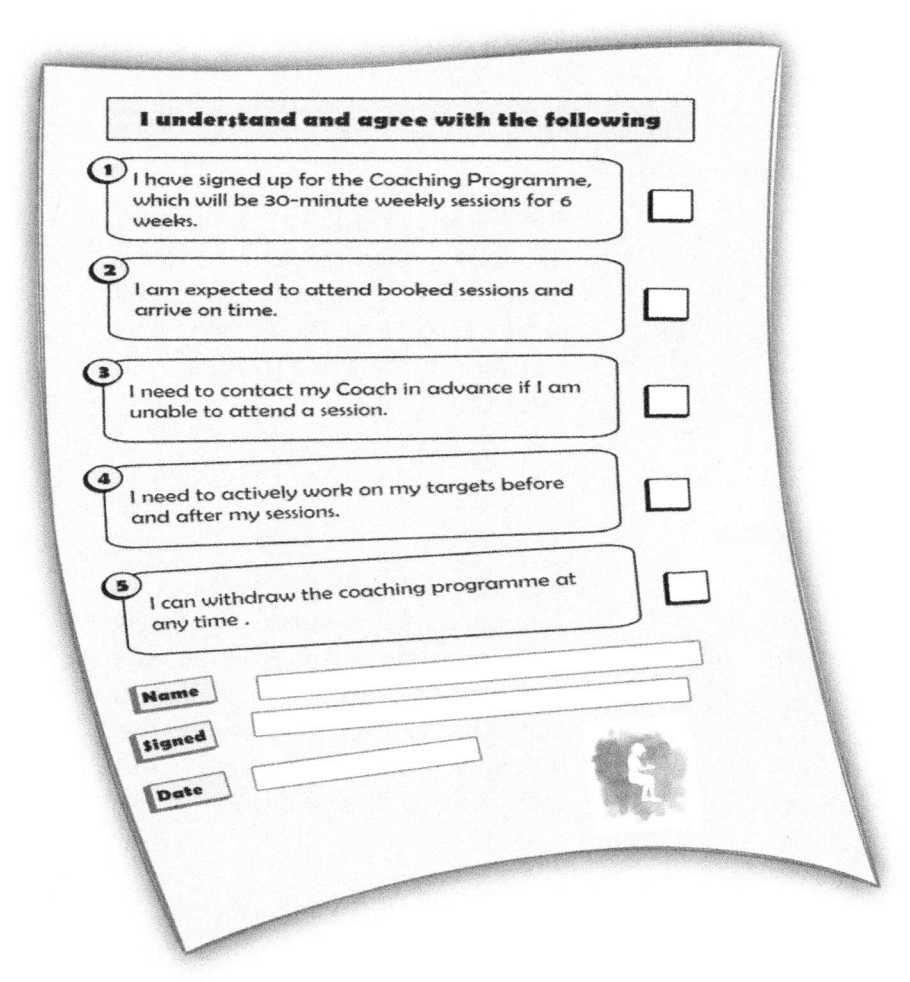

**I understand and agree with the following**

1. I have signed up for the Coaching Programme, which will be 30-minute weekly sessions for 6 weeks.
2. I am expected to attend booked sessions and arrive on time.
3. I need to contact my Coach in advance if I am unable to attend a session.
4. I need to actively work on my targets before and after my sessions.
5. I can withdraw the coaching programme at any time.

Name
Signed
Date

*Figure 8: Example of consent form*

## The approach before the method

The Relate model was developed with a broader cohort of learners in mind, not with a focus on neurodiversity. However, the essence of its philosophy is an inclusive pedagogy that is centred on the learner's needs, potential and aspirations. Conducting these coaching sessions for a few years with a diverse group of young people gave me the basis to systematise the otherwise informal conversations.

Many neurodivergent young people say they find small talk highly challenging. It is common for them to find informal conversations pointless or unnecessary, unless the topic is one of their special interests. Having that in mind, I anticipated that having a systematic approach to the informal conversations with them would be more successful.

When I first started the chats with Terence, we could go around in circles about his feelings of not belonging in his peer group, his difficulties with staying in a lesson until the end and everything that came with it. The introduction of the book about Asperger's in school was a turning point for us. It gave us a tangible target and a structure for the conversations.

Because Terence could choose the topics from the book, and the way we used the book material was adapted to his needs, we managed to keep the sessions open ended and flexible enough to avoid a prescribed generic approach. When thinking of neurodiversity, moreover diversity as a broader concept, it is essential to keep in mind that a neurodivergent person is not an exception to a rule.

Neurodiversity *is* the rule. Being different is the norm. We have become so comfortable with the educational model that puts several individuals in a group and teaches them as a homogeneous mass that we need to step out of that paradigm to remember that every single young person in every group is unique. Being unique is not a prerogative of an autistic or another neurodivergent person. With that notion in mind, in every opportunity that a young person wants to work on their self-awareness, it is fundamental to adapt any approach to their preferences and tendencies. This is why Relate has worked well because it is adaptable by principle.

One programme that I ran consistently was academic coaching. Once the academic topics had been agreed with the young person, the sessions were planned ahead in a similar fashion that you would do a lesson plan. The following is an example of an initial session plan in which the young person wanted to improve their personal management skills.

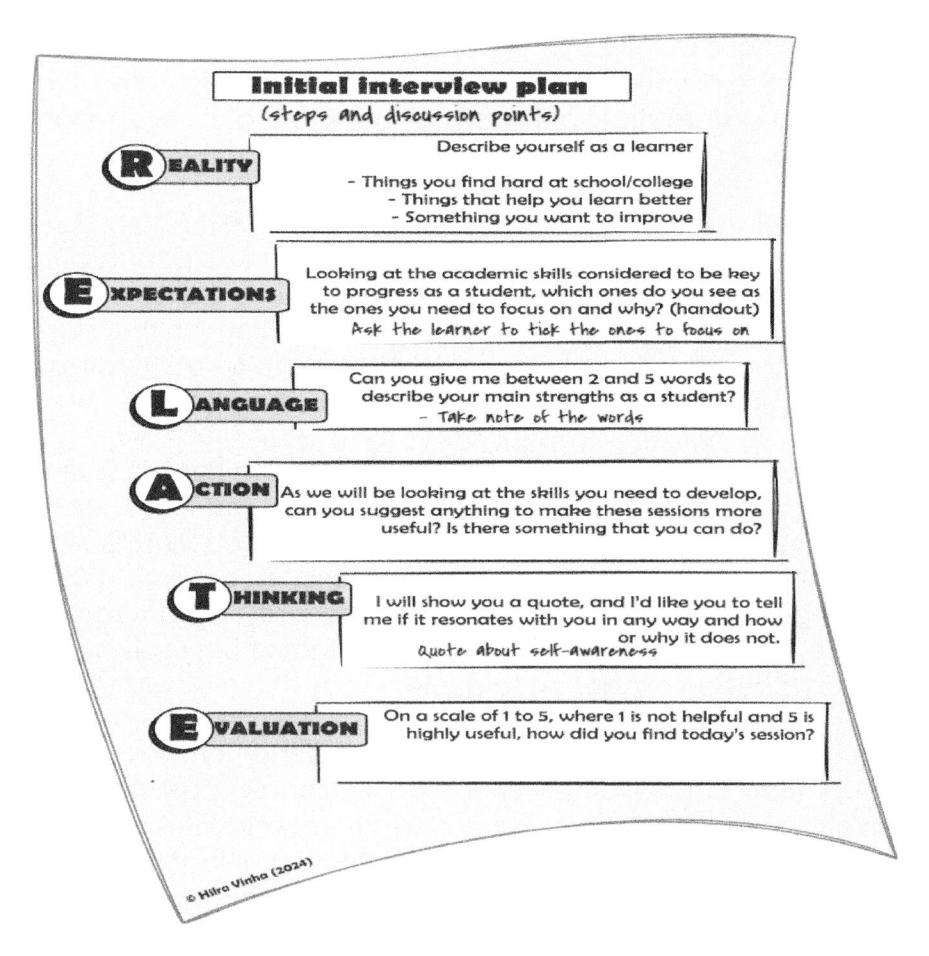

**Initial interview plan**
(steps and discussion points)

**R**EALITY
Describe yourself as a learner
- Things you find hard at school/college
- Things that help you learn better
- Something you want to improve

**E**XPECTATIONS
Looking at the academic skills considered to be key to progress as a student, which ones do you see as the ones you need to focus on and why? (handout)
Ask the learner to tick the ones to focus on

**L**ANGUAGE
Can you give me between 2 and 5 words to describe your main strengths as a student?
- Take note of the words

**A**CTION
As we will be looking at the skills you need to develop, can you suggest anything to make these sessions more useful? Is there something that you can do?

**T**HINKING
I will show you a quote, and I'd like you to tell me if it resonates with you in any way and how or why it does not.
Quote about self-awareness

**E**VALUATION
On a scale of 1 to 5, where 1 is not helpful and 5 is highly useful, how did you find today's session?

© Hilra Vinha (2024)

*Figure 9: Example of interview plan*

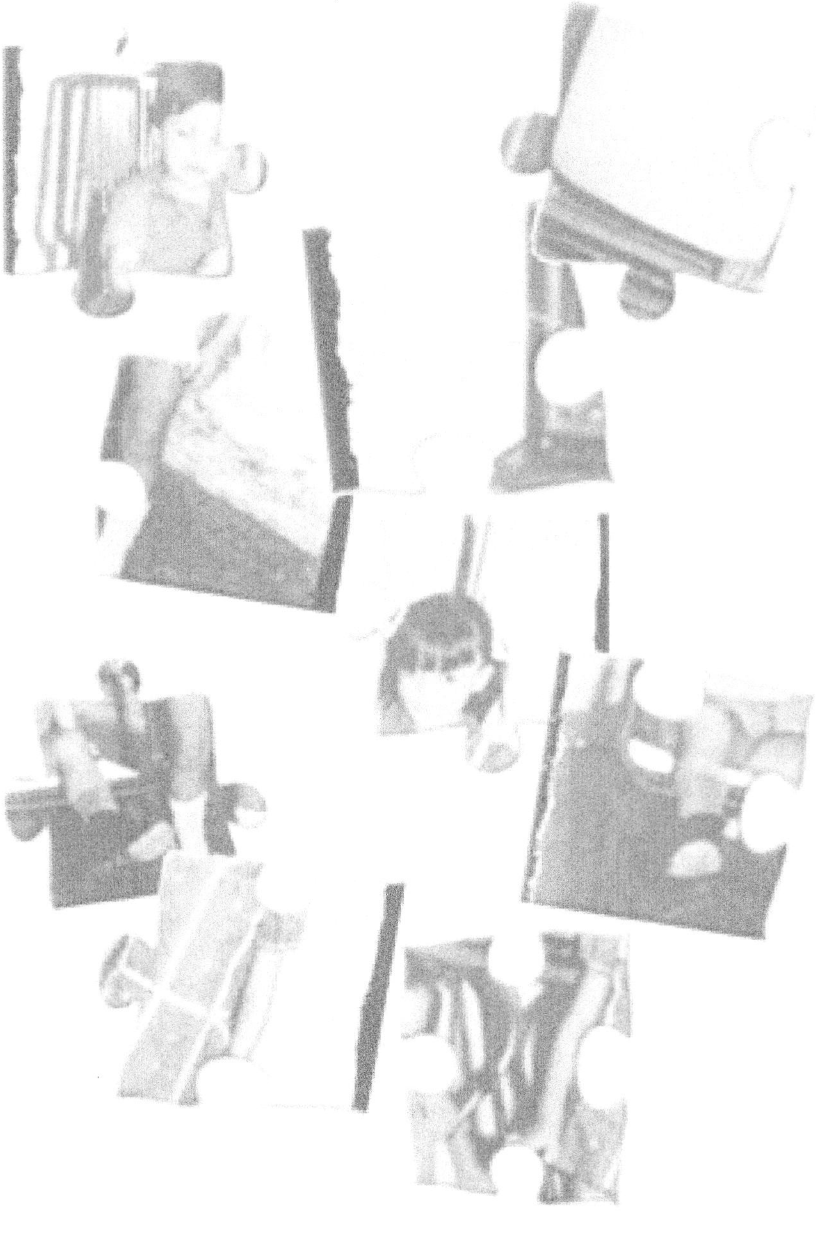

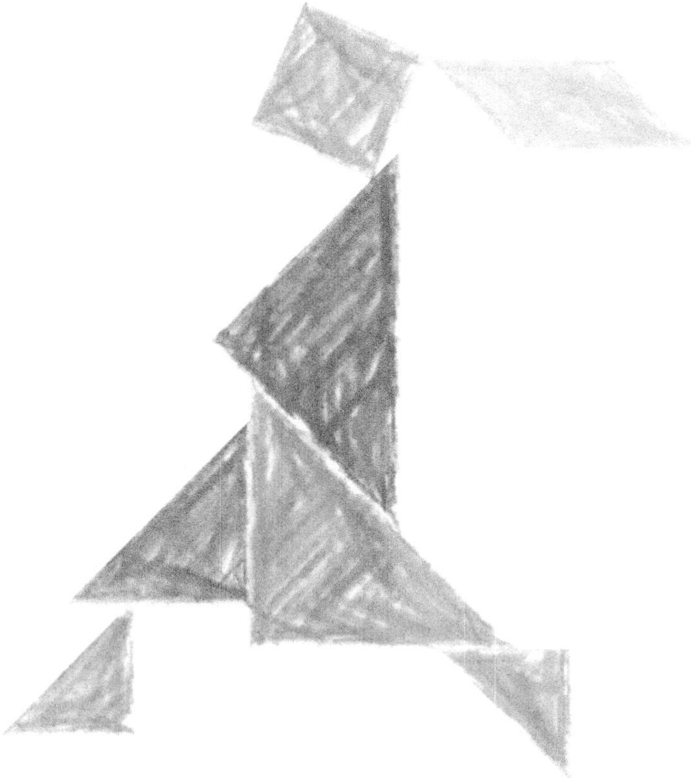

# The Tangram Method

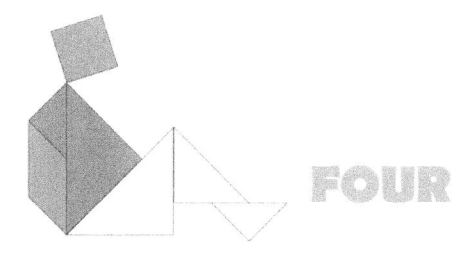

When I carried out my doctoral research, I intentionally chose to adopt open-ended interviews and the notion of the interview process as a conversation to be the essence of my method of inquiry. In my thesis, I explained that my conscious effort to represent the voices of my participants translated into the 'dialogical inquiry' model that I proposed, developed and applied.

Dialogical inquiry is a cycle that starts with the researcher's faith in the participants' capability to actively contribute to the research. The other stages of the cycle are aimed at engaging the participants in a constant dialogue, which means having conversations with the participants and continuously returning to them for a better understanding of what their previous conversations revealed.

The difference between the dialogical inquiry and most other research methods is that the researcher does not try to interpret the data alone. Instead, the participants help with their own interpretations. This method of inquiry was later used in a research project I also became involved with, which looked into the quality of research when done inclusively.

Although my current area of work is not research or teaching, being a trained teacher and researcher reinforces my preference for inquisitive methods and systematisation in my work. Thus, devising this method was a predictable outcome. The autism awareness sessions emerged progressively from learners' needs, as well as my lifelong pedagogical views and research principles. The essential goal of the sessions was the same for all young people: to raise self-awareness.

A better understanding of the masking strategy, the motivation behind it and its consequent emotional labour is a natural subproduct of higher self-awareness in neurodivergent people. From the start, I did not promise I had the answers, nor that the young people would find the answers in these sessions. Instead, I assured them I would cooperatively reflect with them about the issues and the possible routes to a better understanding.

## Learning from their stories

I named this model after my favourite puzzle game because the tangram has always inspired me with its flexibility and countless possibilities. To an extent, these aspects of tangram resonate perfectly with the notion that each person on the autism spectrum has a unique set of traits; and the combination of them creates an individual profile.

Similar to creating pictures with the pieces of the tangram, each person's combination of traits forms a different image, a different recipe. No two neurodivergent people are the same, exactly as no two neurotypical people are.

I propose the Tangram Method is a possible strategy for raising self-awareness in neurodivergent young people in a timely, accessible and efficient manner.

I share with you the main essence of the method, which brings simultaneously the objectives and principles of the method embedded in each stage. The seven principles in action are:

- talking
- analysing
- normalising
- growing
- reconciling
- accepting
- moving on.

I was reluctant to call this approach a 'method'; firstly, because of my research background, I was afraid this could be mistaken as a research method and, secondly, because of the approach having evolved from Relate. I also feared it could be confused with another coaching method. However, I overcame my doubts and fears and decided that the best description to what I had developed was a method, a conversation method or an approach to have methodical conversations.

This dialogical method is based on principles that guide the procedures, which are adaptable to individual needs. The seven principles work as a compass guiding – but not limiting – the necessary adjustments. The facilitator of these methodical conversations must keep the principles in mind at all times to ensure that the young person has plenty of opportunities to experience and actively engage with each one of them. The guiding principles are pointers and reminders of the cognitive movements necessary to awaken self-awareness and realise it. Each action principle opens the door to endless possibilities.

I believe that many young people with a neurodivergent label have been accustomed to knowing and acknowledging their limitations and/or difficulties and all the things that they cannot or would not do.

If we are thinking of an inclusive society where everyone can thrive, we need to change this disabling culture that disseminates endless biases. We must start creating opportunities for all and subsequently everyone will benefit from the outcomes, not only neurodivergent individuals.

Inclusion is not a favour or a kindness gesture that the neurotypically driven society does to the so-called 'disadvantaged' neurodiverse portion of society (no one should be made disadvantaged in the first place), but inclusion is a sustainable strategy to create a better society. A faith in endless possibilities is the essence of the Tangram Method. The neurodivergent person is not a puzzle, nor is their condition.

What is puzzling is the challenge faced by those wanting to change society, to propose new shapes and perhaps a brand-new game. Inviting the young person to engage in **talking** actively and purposely, as well as **analysing** and **normalising**, means giving them time and space to **grow, reconcile** and **accept**, figuring out the shapes they want to create and what they accomplish by doing so, then **move on**. Like in the tangram itself, the pieces are **moveable**, the figures are **not permanent** and you can create **as many new shapes as you can imagine**. Endless possibilities!

Understanding and embracing the seven principles is a key criterion to be able to apply the Tangram Method in conversations with learners. By reading this story, I hope you can take away the notion that you are on a similar trajectory and probably following the right track. At the heart of the method is the active listening to the young person and the application of a set routine centred on the seven principles. Having that basic routine gives the neurodivergent young person the safety of knowing what to expect and what is expected from them in each meeting, while still keeping it flexible. The routine is a safety net, not a strict prescription.

## Talking

One typical occurrence among young people on the spectrum is having difficulties with communication. Some can be overly talkative for lacking the skills to read body language and other nonverbal signals that indicate that the other person wants to say something, change subject or finish the conversation.

Some others may find it hard to translate their thoughts into words or find it hard to speak up due to social anxieties. You may also find that some young people can be talkative on certain days or in some situations then unable to utter a word on other occasions. The invitation to engage in **talking** is an essential part of the Tangram Method, because it creates the dialogical space. Consequently, to fulfil that principle, the facilitator will need to be guided by the young person's communication style to decide which techniques and activities can be trialled.

Because language is a communication device but also a learning tool, humans learn and consolidate learning by using language (verbally or not), **conversation** is the essence of the method itself. However, this can take many formats.

Terence personifies the talking principle as his story was the initial motivation to start an open conversation about autism and his school experience. For the most part of our interactions, Terence saw our sessions simply as an opportunity to talk. Talking was the way Terence organised his understanding of his emotions. It was by talking that he tested his theory of mind, showing a genuine interest in understanding others and their thoughts and feelings.

## Analysing

The primary aim of the sessions is to foster self-awareness to improve wellbeing and reduce struggles, including the avoidable misused energy involved in masking. Carefully considering events, reactions to situations, preferences and dislikes can have a significant role in developing a positive self-image and increasing self-acceptance.

As the young person talks, sharing impressions, telling stories, commenting on events and people, the role of the adult facilitator is to actively and purposefully listen and continuously ask reflexive questions, promoting constant self-questioning and self-awareness. In most cases, the young person will not have an immediate answer or may not be able to articulate one. Which is not a problem, because the actual objective here is the reflection not finding answers. Frequently, a few sessions later, the young person would come back to an old question and discuss their thoughts. This exercise of going away and thinking about the questions is the desired and crucial analysis. That is what you invite them to do.

Albert embodies the analysing principle. His scientific tendencies to search for causality and his quest to comprehend complex aspects of his autism permitted me to have an insight into his discoveries and conclusions based on systematic analysis.

Simply talking about emotions would not interest Albert. While rationally and pragmatically analysing those same emotions made sense and allowed him to extrapolate the analysis and accomplish the other principles.

## Normalising

In the past decade, I have had numerous conversations with autistic young people and their parents. As I mentioned earlier, my researcher mind tends to spot patterns. A constant in these conversations has been the autistic people perceiving themselves as a type of outcast; some will use words like 'weird' to describe themselves. Having grown up as the abled sister of a disabled brother in a society that did not embrace difference, I am familiar with this sense of not belonging and being an outcast. It made me also a strong advocate for **normalising** differences.

My little brother is now a middle-aged man, who still is a boy at heart and mind. Embracing his differences, honouring his abilities and promoting the development of a world where he is not a second-class citizen is what is behind everything I do. To

**normalise** difference is not valuing **normality** but rather celebrating **diversity**.

Being uncommon is fabulous, who wants to be average? **Normalise** being unique, having singular tastes, being fans of underground bands that no one knows, setting your own trends instead of following social media ones. The use of the Tangram Method requires maintaining this mindset throughout the conversations.

Nicole embodies the normalising principle because her chief motivation to discuss her sensory issues that caused cognitive overload was necessary to deconstruct notions of abnormality. The strong desire to understand oneself and normalise uniqueness was empowering for Nicole in her journey towards self-awareness.

## Growing

**Growing** in this context refers to becoming more self-aware and having stronger self-acceptance. **Growing** is the objective of these methodical conversations in the first place. I present **growing** as one of the principles as a reminder that growth must be celebrated consistently and often. Each new discovery, insight and realisation – whether life-changing or ordinary – must be valued as part of the process of becoming a better self.

It is crucial to distinguish this type of **growth** from the idea of growing *out* of something or growing *into* something else. The **growing** experienced as a result of raised self-awareness **happens within** self-acceptance and the notion of pushing the personal capabilities to their optimum, trusting that being oneself is not only enough, but it is enormously empowering. I do not consider neurodivergence a superpower. However, I have witnessed and shared experiences of neurodivergence being super-empowering, which is another kettle of fish entirely.

**The Tangram Method**

I say that and Michael Barton comes to mind because of his book title, but also because he is someone who has proven that owning your neurodivergence is empowering to yourself and others. That is the type of **growing** that we focus on when we apply the Tangram Method in conversation.

Georgie epitomises the growing principle because her academic abilities were of such high calibre, that there was no shadow of doubt that her growth was unrelated to overcoming cognitive or behavioural barriers.

Georgie came to our conversations with an admirable level of emotional literacy, which included a robust grasp of the mental health battles experienced by her close friends. Georgie is the perfect example of what growing means in the context of the Tangram Method. Go out there and continue to grow that incredible skill of being oneself. The true and unmasked self.

## Reconciling

By talking, analysing and normalising we must reach some **reconciliation** with ourselves. Every young person who I encountered in a professional capacity displayed some degree of anxiety due to their inconformity with the world and its arbitrary rules. Often the internal and external expectations mismatched their personal preferences and tendencies. The Tangram Method conversations are great opportunities for reconciling the desire to belong and the essential need to stay true to oneself. Many people talk about the importance of fitting in, but in my experience, this is not the main quest of autistic young people, rather it is to belong without having to conform to a stereotype.

This is achieved by **reconciling** contradictions, paradoxes, strengths and weaknesses. An example of these paradoxes is the longing for friendship and the aversion for socialising experienced by many neurodivergent children and young people. To raise self-awareness as a neurodivergent person is to live and breathe differences, which creates conflicting situations, mixed feelings, non-linear thinking and sometimes ambiguous choices.

None of which comes naturally to most autistic individuals; and that is why the method is founded on the principle of encouraging young people to seek to **reconcile** these opposing forces.

Rowan embodies the reconciling principle as their story was the one that initiated the approach of looking at the autistic traits in combination with the personality ones. That was due to the many contradictions we found when talking about Rowan's views, tendencies and personal preferences. Rowan's identity was an arduous construction, filled with contradictions and paradoxes. Reconciling was the way forward. Rowan contributed to this notion of reconciling contradicting concepts about self and identity.

## Accepting

The social history of learning disabilities is packed with examples of rejection, discrimination, segregation and devaluation of individuals for their differences or disabilities. The neurodiversity movement has led several campaigns promoting acceptance in recent years. Centuries of ignorance will take some time to disappear from our collective unconscious biases. **Accepting** takes shape in the method by the constant observance of signs of self-rejection based on lack of acceptance of individual differences.

To become self-aware and reduce or eliminate the need to mask or camouflage starts with the process of **self-acceptance**. Masking is a conscious or subconscious attempt to become someone different, someone perceived as more acceptable. If a young person feels accepted, if they accept themselves and their neurodivergence, the need to mask becomes obsolete because being oneself becomes enough. The acceptance principle means 'being you is enough'.

Ace exemplifies the accepting principle because a central part of his awareness sessions revolved around reflections about self-acceptance and the acceptance of others, which Ace found extremely challenging.

Ace also struggled with accepting things that did not make sense to him. Much of Ace's conversations revolved around his annoyance with the things he disapproved of or disliked. For that reason, challenging those feelings and the need to accept other views and other ways was a constant in his conversations.

## Moving on

The ultimate goal of the Tangram Method is to promote conversations that encourage and enable young people to move on. Some see **moving on** as transitioning to adulthood, getting a job, going to university or starting a family. For others, **moving on** means stopping feelings of inadequacy, then masking half the time and dealing with the heavy consequences of it the other half. Considering that these conversations tend to start from a point where the young person reached out for help, an essential component of its efficacy lays on the commitment to challenge the young person, to ask difficult questions, to play devil's advocate sometimes and constantly push them to **move on**.

Max embodies the moving on principle because from start to finish, his awareness sessions focused on coping with transitions in life, progressing to new stages and literally moving on and away. Max epitomises the idea of raising self-awareness to move on.

An incredible example of this was our discussions around idioms and his resistance to accept some sayings that seemed absurd, like the classic 'it's raining cats and dogs'. I shared my experience as a speaker of a second language, how I had to learn the history behind some idioms that do not translate to my culture. In the next meeting, Max had learned many historical facts about idioms. He had moved on from being defeated by them, to questioning and then to embracing them.

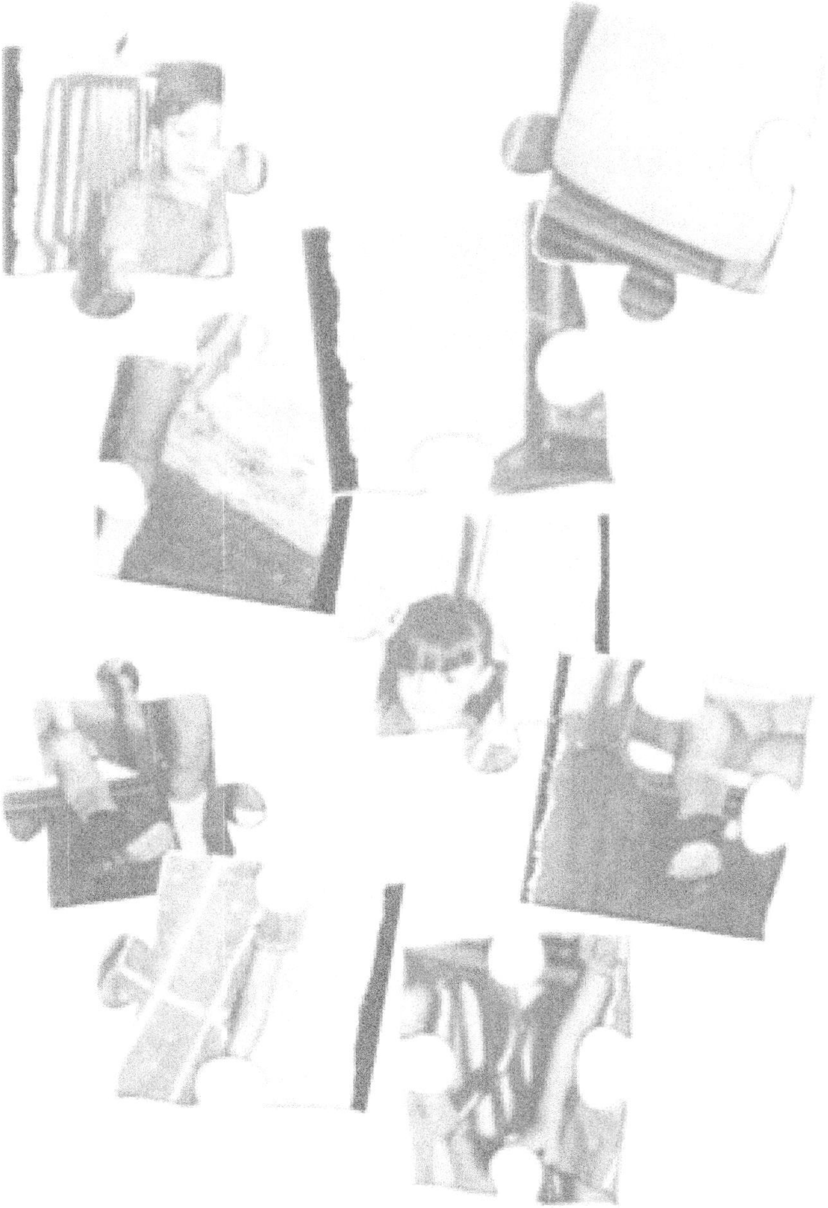

# FIVE

# Takeaways

I hope that at this point in your reading you have realised this is the story of how several different young people on the autism spectrum taught me about autism. I describe how I took stock of these experiences and the ideas I came up with at each situation and how they worked out for each individual. It is also a record of what happened to those seven young people after we completed a period of regular conversations.

My wish is for this book to give you some ideas and the motivation to take inspiration from those young people and implement some of the ideas I tried out. In this chapter, I try to put together a concise overview of the Tangram Method, but most importantly, an outline of a work-in-progress mindset.

We are all work in progress. This idea should free us from perfectionism and any other belief that restricts our freedom to innovate and create momentum.

We need a world that has enough scope and opportunities for neurodiversity and celebration of neurodivergence. I hope your major takeaway from the time you dedicated to this book is encouragement to go out there and openly advocate for difference. I hope this story helped you in finding the courage to do this.

## Putting it into practice

I have been telling you the story of how I developed the autism awareness sessions which then gave birth to the Tangram Method. I offered you an overview of my thinking process and general approach to what I consider an inclusive practice or at least a practice done more inclusively. Now I want to give you some insight into the practicalities of offering those sessions if you are inspired by this story and encouraged by this method. If you work with young people in a capacity that allows you to advocate for neurodiversity and to be an ambassador for the neurodivergent young people, it is most likely that you have what it takes to lead these methodical conversations.

You will need to consider: your role in relation to the young people; the access you have to their time; how much time you can commit to this work; and how you believe these sessions may be relevant to the young people you work with or support. In the following diagram (Fig. 10), I propose a checklist to help you decide if you are in a position to invite young people to neurodiversity-structured or semi-structured conversations with you.

> Are you the right person to offer conversations using the Tangram Method?

## Things to consider...

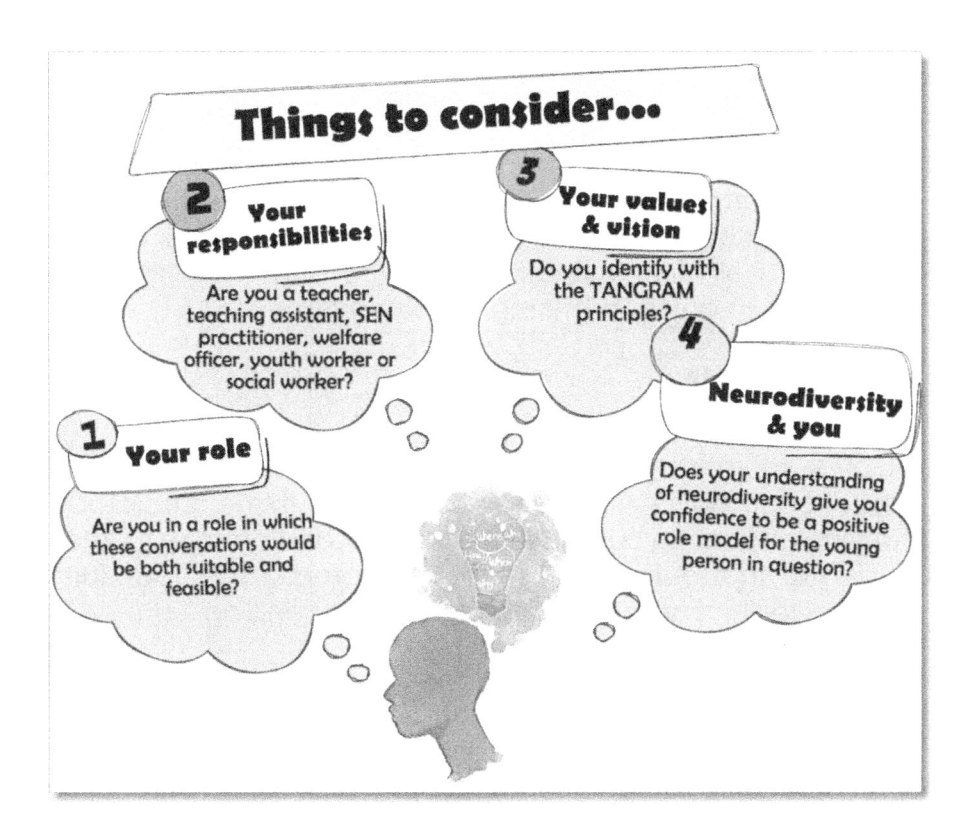

**1. Your role**
Are you in a role in which these conversations would be both suitable and feasible?

**2. Your responsibilities**
Are you a teacher, teaching assistant, SEN practitioner, welfare officer, youth worker or social worker?

**3. Your values & vision**
Do you identify with the TANGRAM principles?

**4. Neurodiversity & you**
Does your understanding of neurodiversity give you confidence to be a positive role model for the young person in question?

*Figure 10: Checking individual suitability*

Once you are confident that using the Tangram Method is appropriate for you and your young people, it is time to plan how you will tailor what you learned here to your young person's needs. Bringing them onboard and fully informed is the first and most critical step.

## Informed consent

Some aspects are fundamental to safeguard the young person and ensure they are informed and capable of agreeing to take part. You may want to consult with parents to make sure it is appropriate to offer the sessions to the young person. This is especially true if the young person in question is less verbal or becomes nonverbal in certain circumstances, because you need to be able to communicate with the young person without creating unnecessary struggles for them.

A clear informed consent form is well evidenced as an effective way to ascertain that you do all checks and give the young person the chance to ask questions and clarify any doubts. Having all points in writing helps you to remember to cover everything, so any consent is given fully informed.

## The predictable

One common challenge faced by autistic people is the difficulty to manage unpredictable events. To address that aspect positively, a strategy I use is to start with the predictable stuff: the elements you can clarify upfront and promise to keep as part of the routine. I list here some predictable facts and events that can be considered depending on your circumstances.

- Day, time and duration of the sessions: once the day and time has been agreed and logistics organised, give that information to the young person in a tangible format, such as via email, electronic calendar invite or a note on a Post-it – whatever works best for you and your young person.
- 30-minute sessions work well for most young people, but some may need longer. Decide at the beginning and stick to it. You can use a timer to make sure you finish the session on time, even if an activity may be left to be finished later.
- Explain that you will use a particular method for these conversations and part of it will be to agree on the duration. Six weeks is a well-tried length for many individual interventions, so I usually start with a six-week plan – with the final session including a review to decide if it is necessary to run another 6-week programme.

## Takeaways

- Have all six dates written down (or on the email you sent with the day and time). You can book all sessions on a shared electronic calendar.
- When offering the individual sessions, be clear about what the topic of the conversations will be. It is a good idea to include that information together with the time and dates of sessions (e.g. 10th March – autism awareness about communication or shutdowns; 17th March – situational nonverbalism).

## The unpredictable

You may be thinking, how can one provide a list of things that are unpredictable? Indeed, that is not an easy task, but it will be highly significant if you can compose a short list of the things you know may happen that are out of your control. Instead of leaving it to chance and expecting the young person to cope if they occur (we cross that bridge when..., and all that), you will prepare them for the *possibility* of the unpredictable (but probable) changes of plan.

- You may need to delay the start of a meeting because a previous meeting may run over time.
- You may have to cancel a meeting at the last minute because you are urgently required elsewhere.
- A meeting may have to be terminated halfway through because you need to respond to an emergency.
- The young person may have a bad day and want to cancel the meeting.
- The young person may want to stop the sessions entirely.
- Acknowledge that some things are so unpredictable that you cannot add them to this list, so it may happen that they will have to improvise at some point.

## Strategies for the seven principles

As I frequently reaffirm, the seven principles are the foundations of every activity and they are almost inseparable. However, the chief principle is the invitation to *talk* given that conversation is the nature of the method itself.

However, speaking can be an issue to a significant number of autistic young people. Bearing that in mind, I have used a few simple but effective strategies to make sure the conversations are adjusted according to each individual.

## The talking principle with the overly talkative

By the point that you have invited a young person to the sessions, you should know their communication style. The overly talkative may need you to adjust your approach to make sure they speak freely and also practise listening and interchanging ideas. However, you must avoid any strategy that may lead to masking. The point here is to encourage them to engage in **talking** and adjusting the interchanges in a way that is fair for both of you. Things you can agree at the start to help with this are:

- Tell them the session is for their benefit and you want to hear their thoughts, ideas, questions and even verbal ramblings. But check with them if they would like to be given a clear indication to when you need to interrupt them or to switch turns.

- They can suggest a sign or gesture you will use to let them know you need to speak. Use this as often as you feel necessary, but only if you really have something relevant to say, not merely as a means to *teach* them to take turns. That is not the aim here.

- Explain that, because you may not want to interrupt their train of thought, you may take some notes while they are

## Takeaways

speaking, so you can refer to them when they've finished. You may refrain from making it too obvious, but do not conceal your notes. Find the balance between making it blatant that you are taking notes and giving a little silent hint.

- Let them know that sometimes you may be taking notes because what they are saying is something you want to explore further.

- Make an agreement that when you are the one talking for too long, they will use the same signal to let you know they need to interrupt you. They can also take notes while you speak.

- Most definitely adopt a timer that will tell both of you the session has finished, no matter who is speaking. It should be a case of wrapping up fast and ending or making a note to continue talking about that point next time.

## The talking principle with the less verbal

You will have to assess wisely if this format of session works for your young person. You must already have an open communication channel with them, to be confident that you can hold relevant conversations with them for a number of weeks.

Once you have established good communication with them, you can plan how you are going to keep the conversation meaningful and stimulating for the young person. Although engaging a less verbal person in **talking** is possibly the most challenging scenario, it is also uncomplicated to address. Below are some strategies you can try:

- Use communication cards as a starting point and/or for days in which the young person is nonverbal.

- Incorporate a small whiteboard where they can write their answers to you. You can create your own by laminating an A4 card.

- Use a small notebook or some scrap paper for writing if you do not have access to a small whiteboard.

- Let the young person use their own electronic device to write, if they have a phone or tablet, for instance.

- Turn all your questions into closed questions (yes and no answers) and do not ask compound questions (several questions in one). Ask one thing at a time to allow time to process and possibly answer.

- Be patient. Wait. Do not rush them. Allow the silence for as long as they need. Do not answer for them.

- After a long silence that you realise will not turn into an answer, free them up from your question by saying it is OK for them to answer another time. Reassure them it is not a problem, you will get back to the question if you need to. Let go of it for now and move on.

- In no circumstance demand that they speak if they are not speaking. But you can suggest they nod or do thumbs up/down, if they can.

- Let them decide if they'd prefer to cancel the session on that day, in which case you can book a replacement day if they choose that option.

# How to implement the other principles

## Analysing

Propose researching tasks they can do online with some parameters. You may suggest specific websites you know may provide good material for self-reflection. If you have access to books, particularly those written by neurodivergent authors, you can suggest those.

Using the Neurodiversity Cards can be a way to analyse individual preferences, tendencies and ways of thinking. If you feel comfortable explaining the personality types, you can also use that strategy as I describe later in this chapter.

## Normalising

Normalising requires a mindset not a strategy. Simply use every opportunity to **celebrate difference**, to remind them that the golden rule of diversity is that it is *normal* to be different. What is *not* normal is to be *the same* as somebody else. Even identical twins have their individualities. Some things you could discuss with them are:

- Famous neurodivergent people in history
- Current neurodivergent influencers and experts (You can find online annotated lists of names and links that can be helpful.)
- Famous people with unusual talents who are neurotypical (Show them that being different is normal, neurodivergent or not.)

## Growing

This is another principle that requires an attentive mindset, not a strategy. Practise attention by regularly providing responses to what you observe, such as some of the following:

- Celebrate little wins, recognise growth, verbalise praise and affirmation.
- Make sure the young person knows you see them.
- Help them see themselves in a good light.
- Empower self-knowledge, reaffirm self-worth, focus on self-awareness.

## Reconciling

The reconciliation of opposing views can be a challenge if the young person presents a rigid mindset. But be prepared to challenge their fixed mindset by reminding them of the contradictions that they inheritably experience. It is important that they embrace these contradictions and learn to make peace with them to be themselves freely, without masks. Some of the examples below will resonate with some of the young people:

- The desire to have friends but disliking social contact or finding it exhausting

- The dislike of social situations and the sentiment of loneliness making them sad

- The ability to see details that most people miss, but missing things everyone seems to know without effort

- Having strict opinions about certain subjects by being black or white, right or wrong, good or bad; conversely, being gender fluid, nonbinary or having a taste for combining opposing fashion trends

- Being perfectly proficient in speaking, reading and writing – but lacking good grades in English; being great at mental maths but not able to show the workings of a solution

These are examples of many contradictions that some neurodivergent people might experience without seeing them as contradictions or paradoxes. Try to identify the ones specific to your young person and analyse them together, discussing any difficulties they may face because of their opposing forces.

Encourage them to accept that paradoxes exist and one can make peace with them. Each person finds their own ways to find this reconciliation. You are there just to encourage them to search for that peace, which will most likely be different from yours.

## Accepting

Actions that can support the exercise of self-acceptance can be hard to exemplify, but there are simple strategies that can reflect it through self-disclosure. Once one accepts oneself, disclosure becomes possible such as in the examples below.

- Joining a self-advocacy group or a special interest club

- Volunteering or working in the third sector to help other neurodivergent people

- Taking stock of strategies to avoid sensory overload, cognitive blocks, shutdowns and other outcomes that can be avoided or reduced by acknowledging they may happen and thereby minimising risks

- Choosing your preferred language and letting others know (i.e. autistic person, neurodivergent, person with autism, person on the autism spectrum)

- Helping others to understand the condition better so they can also improve their acceptance

- Carrying a neurodiversity disclose card to help other people to deal with individual needs in a crisis (e.g. the card about tics in the communication card set).

## Moving on

At the initial stages of the discussions about starting the programme, it must be clear what the young person is hoping to gain from the session, as this will keep the expectations realistic and will give a parameter to assess if the conversations are gearing towards the objective of moving on.

Although the **moving on** principle might imply the end of the process, in practical terms the strategy is to plan for it from the start. Below are some points you could cover in the discussion.

- Agree on tangible ways to assess if moving on is in progress.
- Discuss what could indicate they know when this is achieved.
- How will you both know after six weeks if the sessions should continue or stop?
- Create a checklist to use in the sixth week to help the review.

## The neurodiversity cards

### Theory of mind and executive function

Many studies have investigated the relationship between the Theory of mind (Lecheler, 2021) and executive function (Lukito, S., 2017) in the prevalence of autistic traits.

**Theory of mind** is the ability to attribute mental states of others such as beliefs, desires, feelings and intentions. **Executive function** controls the integration of cognitive processes such as: planning; prioritising; directing attention; mental flexibility; multitasking; time management; and metacognition.

I believe that language continues to mediate learning throughout our lives, therefore, encouraging conversations about metacognition are critical to the Tangram approach to promoting autism self-awareness. In my experience, young people appreciate this activity and invest their cognitive drive into making sense of the cards; they search for their own thoughts, feelings and impressions of each situation described and take time and space to appreciate the language that validates them.

## Takeaways

To foster such mediation, I developed the neurodiversity cards focusing on theory of mind and executive function as a conversation starter and self-reflection supporting device.

It appears to me that most young people relish the power to voice what they perceive as their identity and differentiate it from what they see as alien to them. Another reaction I observed repeatedly was an eye-opening gasp after reading a description they felt has actually put into words something they knew but had not articulated themselves.

Selecting the cards based on how they identify with their descriptions provides a golden opportunity to encourage such reflection and to provide affirmation where necessary.

The **neurodiversity awareness** card game consists of three types of cards:

- four cognitive functions presented as pairs including a definition and an example of challenges that can be faced by neurodivergent individuals
- four subsets of eight cards each, comprising those four cognitive functions presented through examples of skills and challenges
- ten extra cards describing some neurodivergent behaviours (see Cards map).

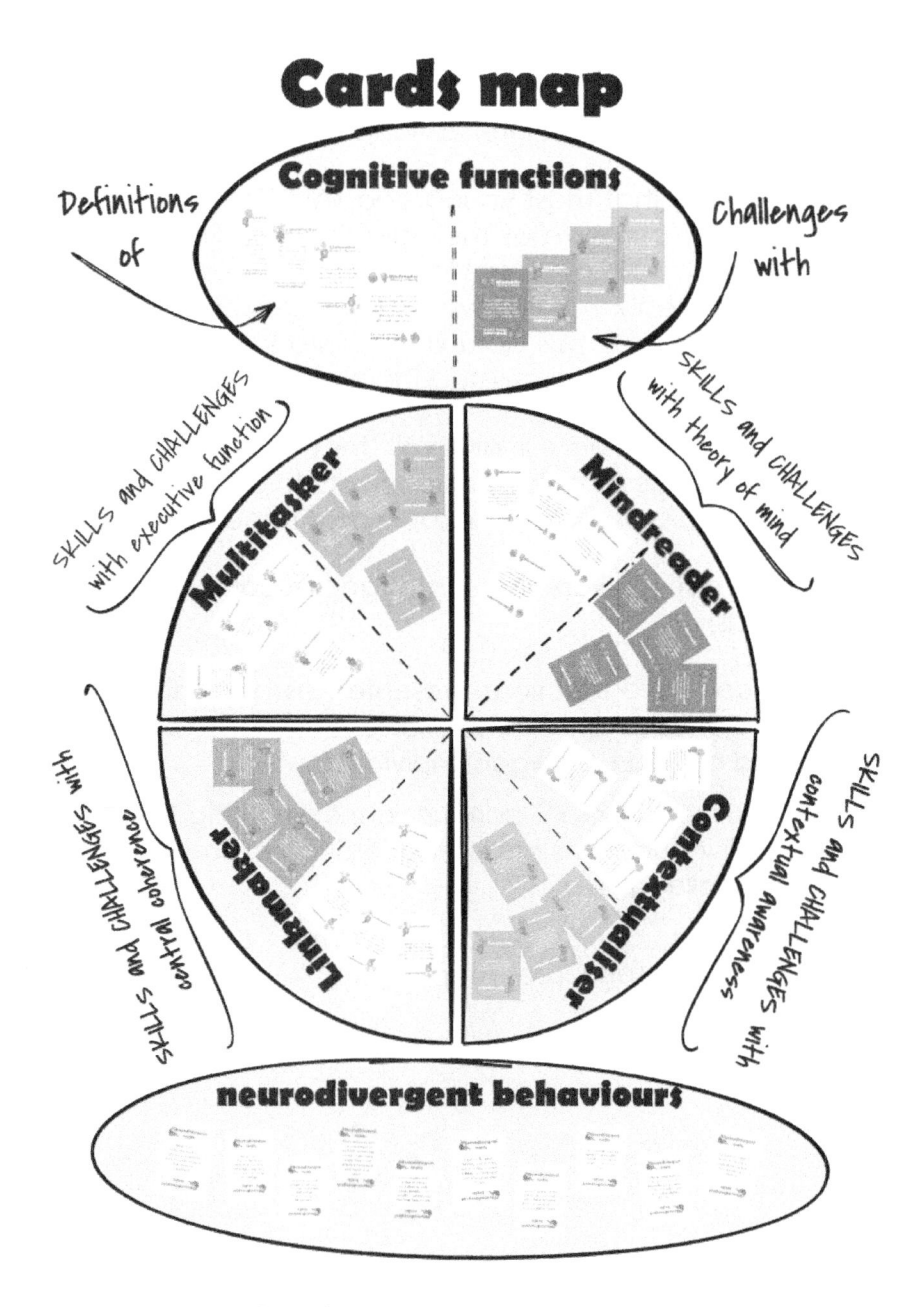

*Figure 11: Visual representation of the set of neurodiversity cards by type*

## Takeaways

The first type of cards, cognitive functions, is used to raise awareness of brain function and increase understanding of the challenges that the young person may face. Each cognitive function is presented in a simplified definition accompanied by a common challenge associated with it.

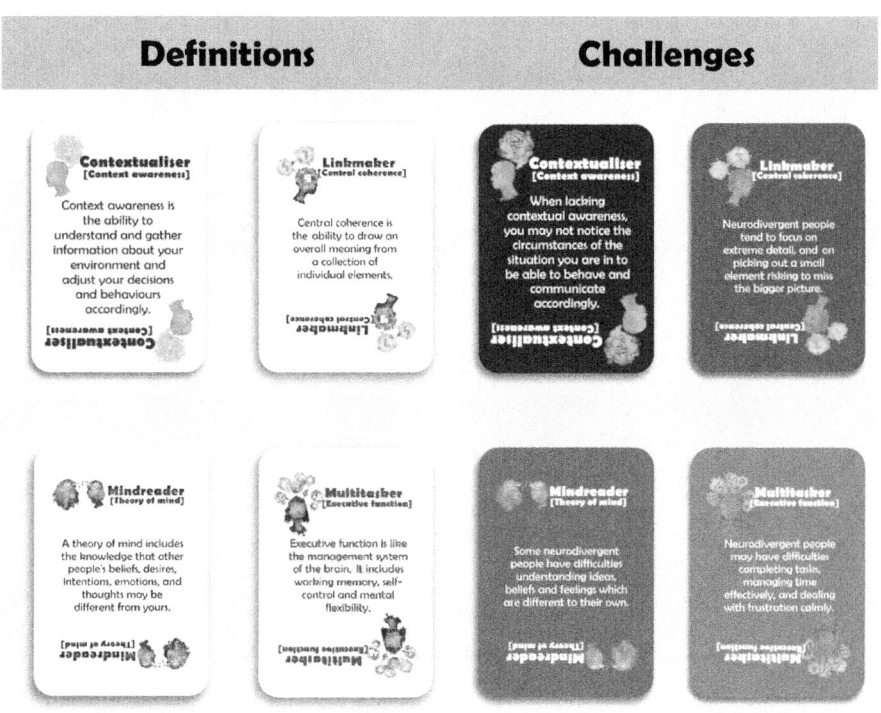

| Definitions | Challenges |
|---|---|
| **Contextualiser** [Context awareness]: Context awareness is the ability to understand and gather information about your environment and adjust your decisions and behaviours accordingly. | **Contextualiser** [Context awareness]: When lacking contextual awareness, you may not notice the circumstances of the situation you are in to be able to behave and communicate accordingly. |
| **Linkmaker** [Central coherence]: Central coherence is the ability to draw an overall meaning from a collection of individual elements. | **Linkmaker** [Central coherence]: Neurodivergent people tend to focus on extreme detail, and on picking out a small element risking to miss the bigger picture. |
| **Mindreader** [Theory of mind]: A theory of mind includes the knowledge that other people's beliefs, desires, intentions, emotions, and thoughts may be different from yours. | **Mindreader** [Theory of mind]: Some neurodivergent people have difficulties understanding ideas, beliefs and feelings which are different to their own. |
| **Multitasker** [Executive function]: Executive function is like the management system of the brain. It includes working memory, self-control and mental flexibility. | **Multitasker** [Executive function]: Neurodivergent people may have difficulties completing tasks, managing time effectively, and dealing with frustration calmly. |

*Table 1: Definitions and concepts*

These four cognitive functions make up the essence of the four main card suits each named after a function: the **Multitasker** (executive function), the **Mindreader** (theory of mind), the **Linkmaker** (central coherence) and the **Contextualiser** (contextual awareness). The deck of cards also includes ten cards related to some common behaviours which some neurodivergent people experience. The objective of these cards is to support the young person in their self-acceptance through understanding the roots of the behaviours and encourage unmasking.

**Theory of mind** — **Executive function**

| The mindreader | The linkmaker | The multitasker | The contextualiser |
|---|---|---|---|
| These cards encourage the young person to reflect on how they understand others and their ways of thinking. | Self-assessing executive functioning is complex, but these cards offer scenarios to help with that. | Multitasking in terms of executive functioning involves transitioning between tasks. These cards offer self-reflection on that. | Contextualising makes things relative and less rigid. These cards reflect on how the young person deals with context. |

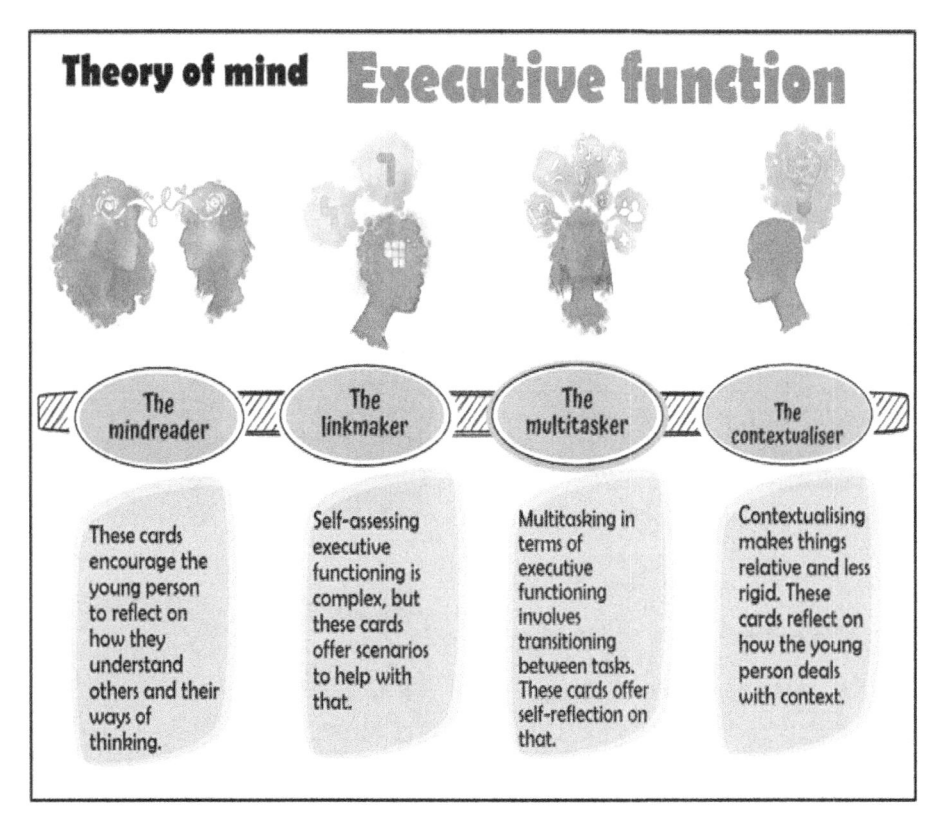

*Figure 12: The cards and their relation to theory of mind and executive function*

As part of this conversation, it is necessary to recognise the external factors that can be challenging and, in turn, identify empowering strategies to deal with these external factors, for example, by reducing or removing barriers. Some empowering strategies are:

- noise-cancelling headphones, shade glasses, fidget toys, walks in green spaces, power naps after sensory overload
- time-out cards, quiet spaces, downtime, silent discos, individually developed strategies

- use of literal and unambiguous language by interlocutor (including parents, teachers, carers, close friends), learning idioms and nonverbal language conventions linked to one's interests.

## The neurodivergent recipe

Since creating this card game to replace the Ryuu, its use in the sessions followed the same approach I had devised for the previous cards. The young person selects the cards with which they identify and discard the ones they do not. The result is what I call their 'individual recipe of traits', which lately I have combined with their personality traits based on their type and the impact of personal experience.

## The neurodivergent traits

The ultimate goal of the self-awareness conversations is to empower autistic young people to make informed decisions about their life and future. Therefore, having a good understanding of their ways of thinking and relationships with others, as well as their environment, is a key part of the whole process.

Based on my observations, choosing the cards that contain their preferences and tendencies gives the young person a sense of validation and normalisation, as opposed to inadequacy and abnormality. The neurodivergent traits can include specific autistic tendencies, combined with any other neurodivergent factors such as difficulties with focused and/or distributed attention, phonological processing or spatial awareness.

## Jung typology

Carl Jung was the founder of analytical psychology in the early twentieth century. Analytical psychology was then a new form of studying the human mind and behaviour. According to Jung, people can be characterised by preferences and attitudes in two main types, depending on how they direct their energy, **extraversion (E)** and **introversion (I)**.

## The Tangram Method

Extraverts[2] gain energy from social interactions while introverts lose energy in social contact. Within those two poles, he described four types depending on how people predominantly perceive and process information.

Perceiving information predominantly by **sensing (S)** or **intuition (N)**

- **Sensing** relates to processing information received predominantly by the senses as in seeing, hearing, touching and tasting.
- **Intuition** relates to having understandings that cannot be explained by the use of the senses, but by intuitive logic.

Processing information predominantly by **thinking (T)** or **feeling (F)**

- **Thinking** relates to processing information predominantly by the rationalisation of intellectual logic.
- **Feeling** relates to processing information predominantly based on how they generate an emotional response.

Jung described eight possible personality types (Fig. 13).

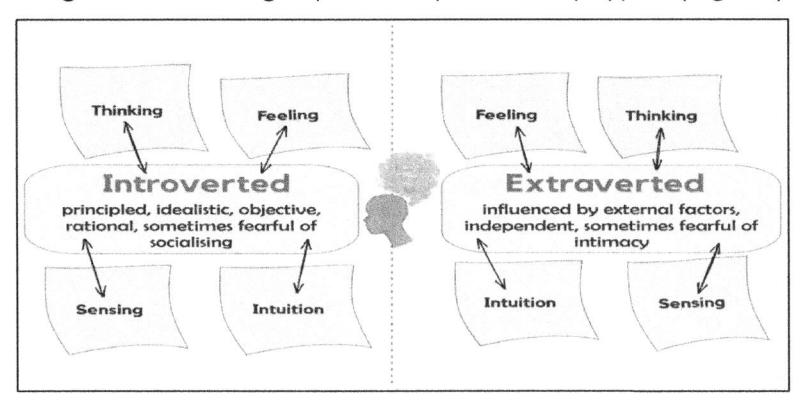

*Figure 13: Jung typology diagram*

---

[2] Nowadays the terms are more commonly spelled extroversion and extrovert.

Later, Isabel Briggs-Myers added another aspect to the personality type: how people use the information once received and processed. She argued that it is by **judging (J)** or **perceiving (P)**.

After this addition, more combinations became possible, so now we have sixteen personality types, commonly referred to as the **Jung and Briggs-Myers** typology. Personality types are based on personal preferences; the combination of choices in each of the main four elements is indicative of behaviours and ways to relate to others and the world.

I am convinced that the juxtaposition of a person's personality type and their prevalent autistic traits can be insightful in their process of self-knowledge, if not taken in a deterministic manner. In addition, I observed that some young people valued looking at personality traits as a way of analysing the broader aspects of their identity that contribute to their behaviour and ways of thinking, beyond and regardless of the diagnosis of a neurodiverse condition.

## Bodily centred aspects

Physical and sensory individual characteristics play a significant role in how we behave and relate to the environment and fellow humans. This is no different for neurodivergent individuals. Consequently, when trying to understand neurodivergence to help to raise self-awareness, it is crucial to consider how physical aspects, such as health, mobility, present conditions and general fitness affect a person's life.

Similarly, the sensory interactions with the world, and all of its stimuli, have a significant influence on how a person experiences neurodivergent traits, personality characteristics and the impact of personal experiences, including learned behaviours.

## The impact of personal experiences

Being neurodivergent can be a challenge to children and young people. I usually meet them between the ages of fourteen and nineteen, when their experiences have already left a lasting effect on them, ranging from masking habits to trusting or mistrusting adults, along with many other unwanted outcomes in between.

Simultaneously, unbeknown to most people around them, these young people do also develop resilience and sophisticated survival strategies. Their neurodivergent brains use creativity and imagination in less conventional ways, which in consequence can go unnoticed or undervalued by those holding neurotypical expectations. The level of nurture and trauma they may have experienced throughout their young lives unfolds in different degrees of masking habits, self-awareness and trauma-based or nurture-based responsive behaviours.

## Putting it all together

The Tangram Method consists of meaningful conversations that nurture self-awareness and foster a sense of self-worth. Self-awareness, in this context, entails a quest for authenticity, free from masks or façades aimed at conformity or approval. Neurodivergent or not, most of us have experienced putting on a front[3] from time to time. Neurodivergent individuals can benefit from the collaboration with neurotypical allies to navigate the neurotypical world and promote awareness of neurodiversity. This collaboration can reduce the double empathy problem working both ways.

The Tangram Method serves as a valuable tool in facilitating such collaboration and fostering self-awareness that embraces neurodivergence, individual personality traits and the influence

---

[3] The concept of 'front' was described by Erving Goffman, see References.

of personal experiences in shaping one's self-concept and identity.

A key aspect to reduce the double empathy paradigm is a mutuality in learning one another's ways of thinking, feeling and acting. Furthermore, this method challenges outdated stereotypes and stigmas associated with autism and neurodiversity. As someone who appreciates puzzles, jigsaw puzzles in particular, it took me some time to grasp the hidden significance behind the puzzle piece which is a symbol of autism.

As this method evolved, I came to realise another layer of meaning which lies in the objective of the game. Unlike completing a jigsaw puzzle, where success hinges on reproducing an exact image by placing each piece in its predetermined location, the Tangram offers a different approach. With those seven pieces that are neither entirely unique nor identical, the Tangram allows for endless possibilities in creating various shapes through strategic placement, harnessing the beauty of geometry.

### The Tangram Method

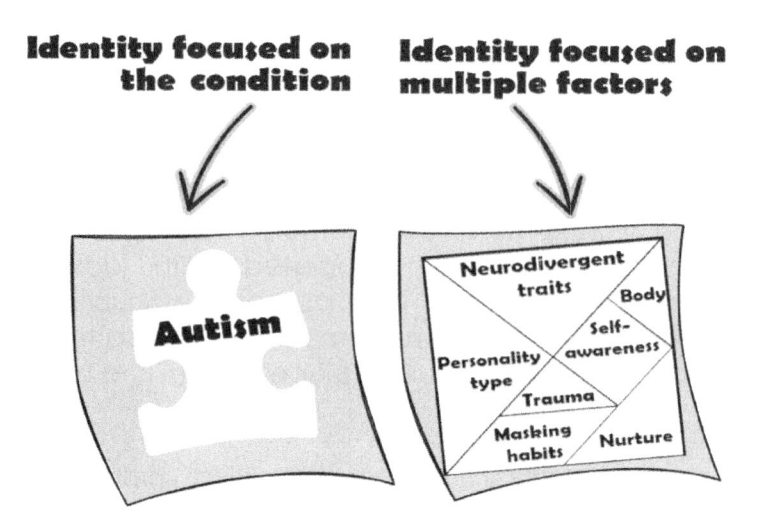

**Identity focused on the condition**

**Identity focused on multiple factors**

*Figure 14: Comparison between different approaches to identity*

In Figure 14, I offer my personal perspective on how each puzzle piece symbolises a person based on their neurodivergence. While the jigsaw piece often symbolises the view that autism defines a person, some individuals and organisations perceive autism as a disorder to be cured or remedied. From the perspective of the Tangram metaphor, a neurodivergent individual is defined by the richness of their experiences, shaped by upbringing and self-awareness of their neurodivergent traits and personality type.

With this in mind, each neurodivergent person can construct their own Tangram to represent themselves if they choose. They can also determine which pieces represent different aspects of themselves, based on the significance they attribute to each aspect in shaping their identity and interactions with the world. Below, I offer my interpretation of how these pieces may be arranged by three different people, depending on their personal experiences and individual characteristics.

- Person A: Neurodivergent traits and personality are predominant in their daily life.

## Takeaways

- Person B: Traumatic experiences and masking strategies are at the fore of everything they do, followed by their bodily centred experiences.
- Person C: Nurturing experiences and high level of self-awareness are the driving forces in their decisions and life choices, with personality playing the next most important role.

### Neurodivergent person A, person B & person C

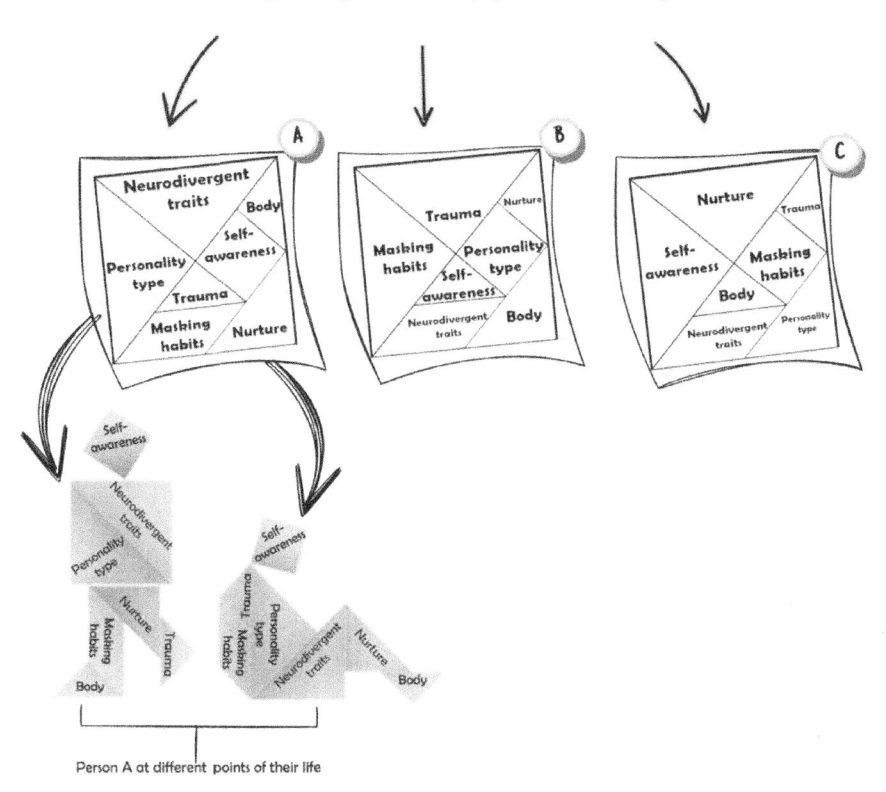

*Figure 15: Visual representation of various autistic profiles*

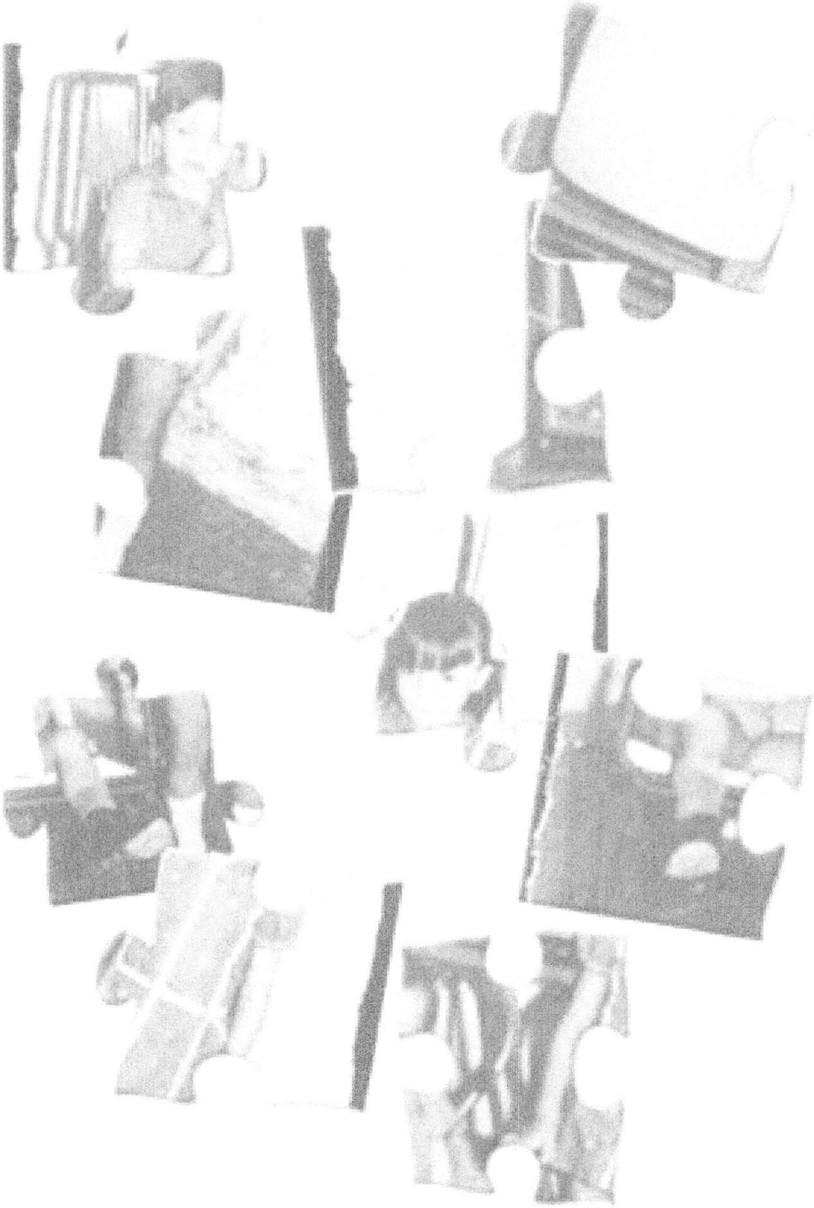

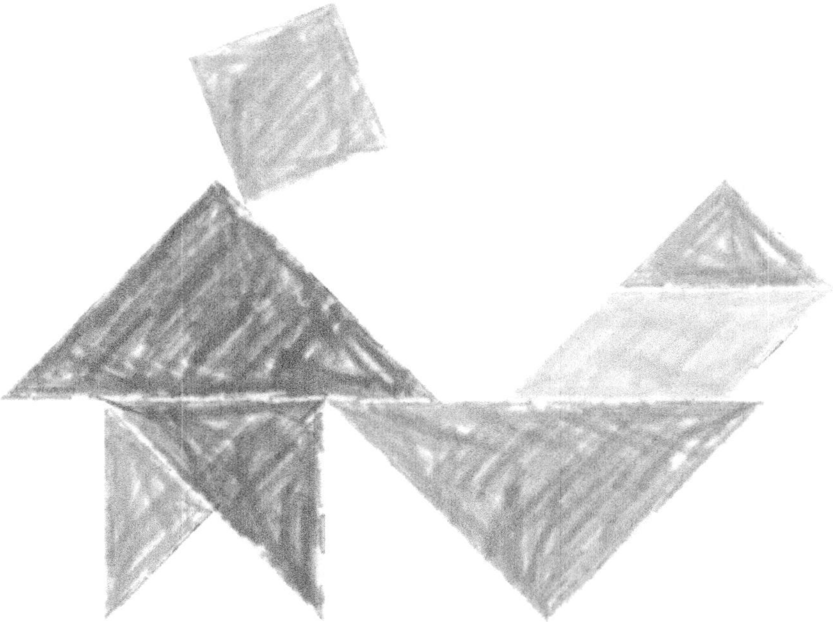

# Shared resources

In this chapter I share a small sample of the materials I have created over the years to support the coaching and the autism awareness sessions. In the following pages you will find examples of activities you can adapt or reuse as they are. Most of them are available to download for free from my website[4].

My purpose in sharing these is to offer tangible proof that fostering self-awareness through conversation is *highly* relevant and equally *highly* simple. I have often discussed matters of inclusion with colleagues who are discouraged from trying to be innovative for fear of not knowing what to do, thinking that it requires special skills. Good will and faith in the young person's ability, greater than doubts about the barriers they face, is what is necessary. If you have those, you will be able to find the appropriate routes to support their journey.

---

[4] hilravinha.com

**The Tangram Method**

## Example of consent form

**I understand and agree with the following**

1. I have signed up for the Coaching Programme, which will be 30-minute weekly sessions for 6 weeks. ☐

2. I am expected to attend booked sessions and arrive on time. ☐

3. I need to contact my Coach in advance if I am unable to attend a session. ☐

4. I need to actively work on my targets before and after my sessions. ☐

5. I can withdraw the coaching programme at any time. ☐

Name
Signed
Date

Shared resources

# **Example of a discussion diagram**

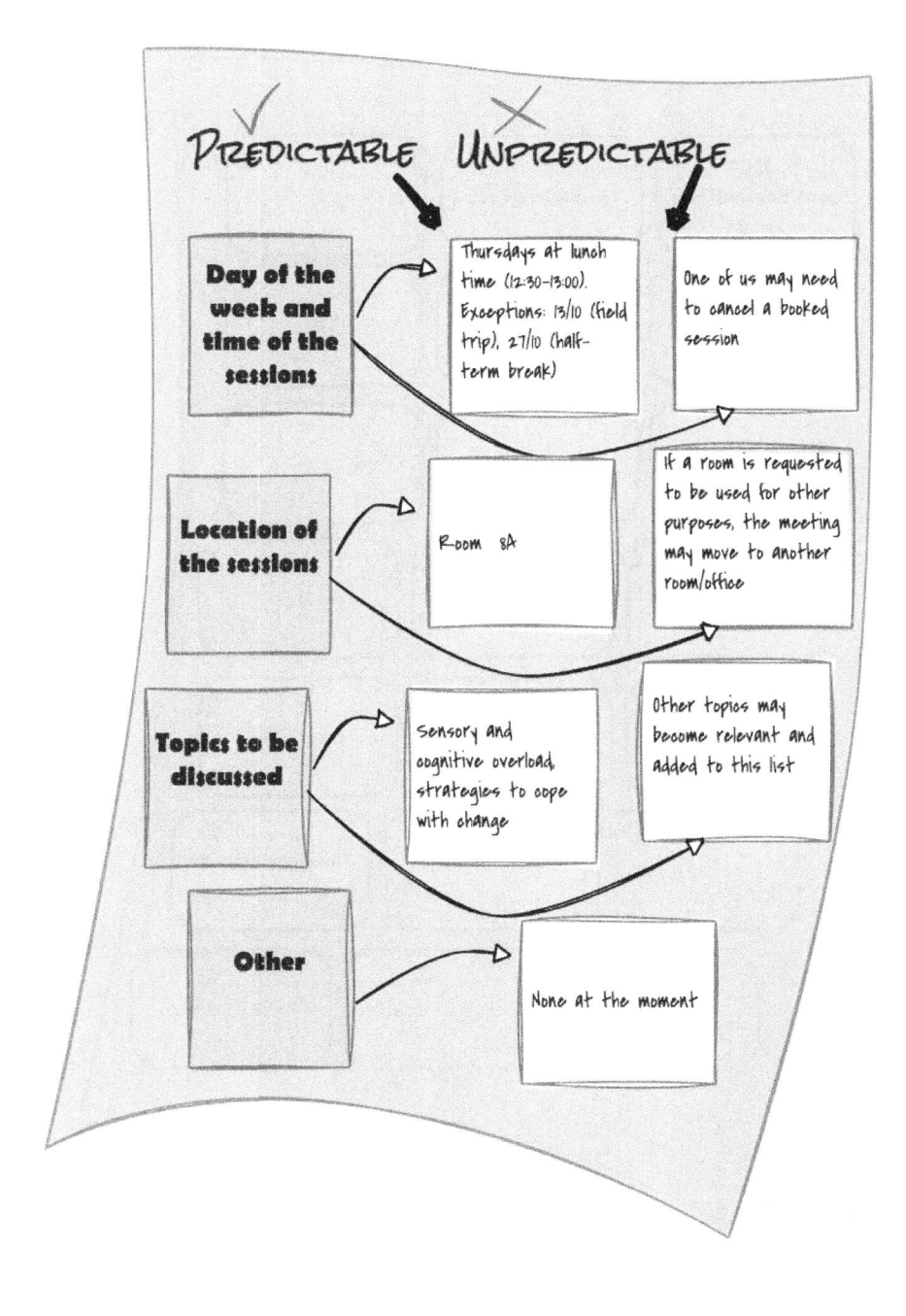

✓ PREDICTABLE   ✗ UNPREDICTABLE

**Day of the week and time of the sessions**
- Thursdays at lunch time (12:30–13:00). Exceptions: 13/10 (field trip), 27/10 (half-term break)
- One of us may need to cancel a booked session

**Location of the sessions**
- Room 8A
- If a room is requested to be used for other purposes, the meeting may move to another room/office

**Topics to be discussed**
- Sensory and cognitive overload, strategies to cope with change
- Other topics may become relevant and added to this list

**Other**
- None at the moment

**The Tangram Method**

# Simplified communication cards

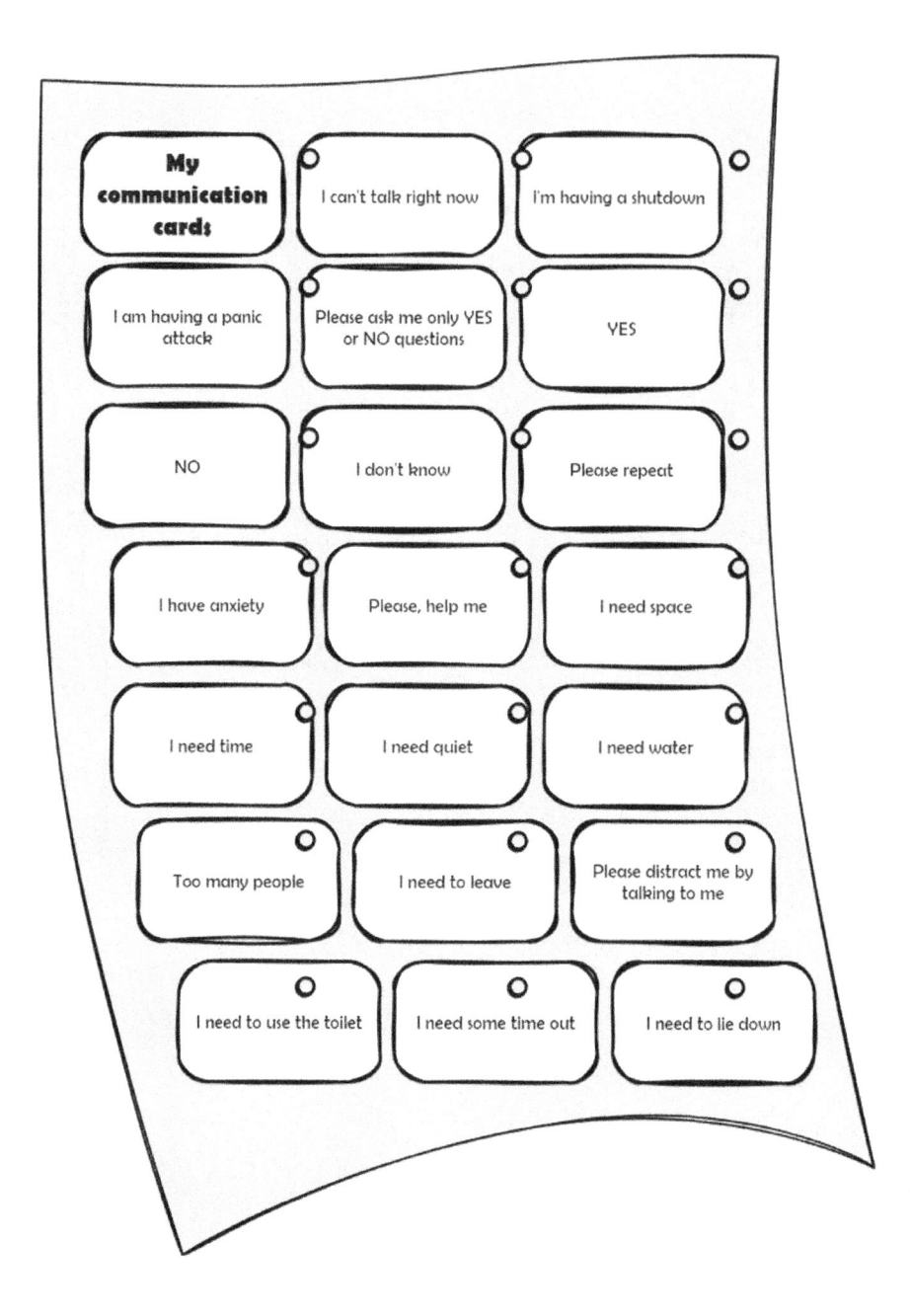

**My communication cards**

- I can't talk right now
- I'm having a shutdown
- I am having a panic attack
- Please ask me only YES or NO questions
- YES
- NO
- I don't know
- Please repeat
- I have anxiety
- Please, help me
- I need space
- I need time
- I need quiet
- I need water
- Too many people
- I need to leave
- Please distract me by talking to me
- I need to use the toilet
- I need some time out
- I need to lie down

# Improving social skills and avoiding masking

We need social skills to get along with others, as well as to create and maintain satisfying relationships. Good social skills can lead to positive social reinforcement, enhancing our self-esteem. Social skills are essential not just in school, but also outside school and later on in the workplace. Like any skills, social skills can be learned and improved. Neurodivergent children and young people can face particular difficulties in this area, mostly due to social expectations of what is acceptable, what is polite and what is impolite. Hence school staff and parents can make systematic efforts to teach them good social skills.

Despite the many positive aspects of good social skills, the pursuit of the standard behaviour that is socially accepted has caused many neurodivergent young people to develop some masking strategies, consciously or not, to survive the struggle. Introvert neurotypical people also develop masking strategies, also known as putting on a 'front'.

Regardless of the terminology, self-acceptance can be impaired by this constant desire to be like others, to be like somebody else, to be other than oneself to meet some external expectation. It is imperative to anyone working with young people to be aware of the importance of validating them, even when they need some constructive feedback or tough love.

Helping the young person to improve any skills cannot mitigate their ability to be their own self. Therefore, whenever social skills matters come to the fore, that reflection becomes necessary. Only after acknowledging the acceptance principle and the resulting reconciliation, does it become valid to discuss social skills as something that can be learned or improved. Below is an example of a handout you can adapt according to your young person's needs, age and preferences. It is meant only as an inspiration, but you can reuse it as is, if you wish.

## Example of self-assessment

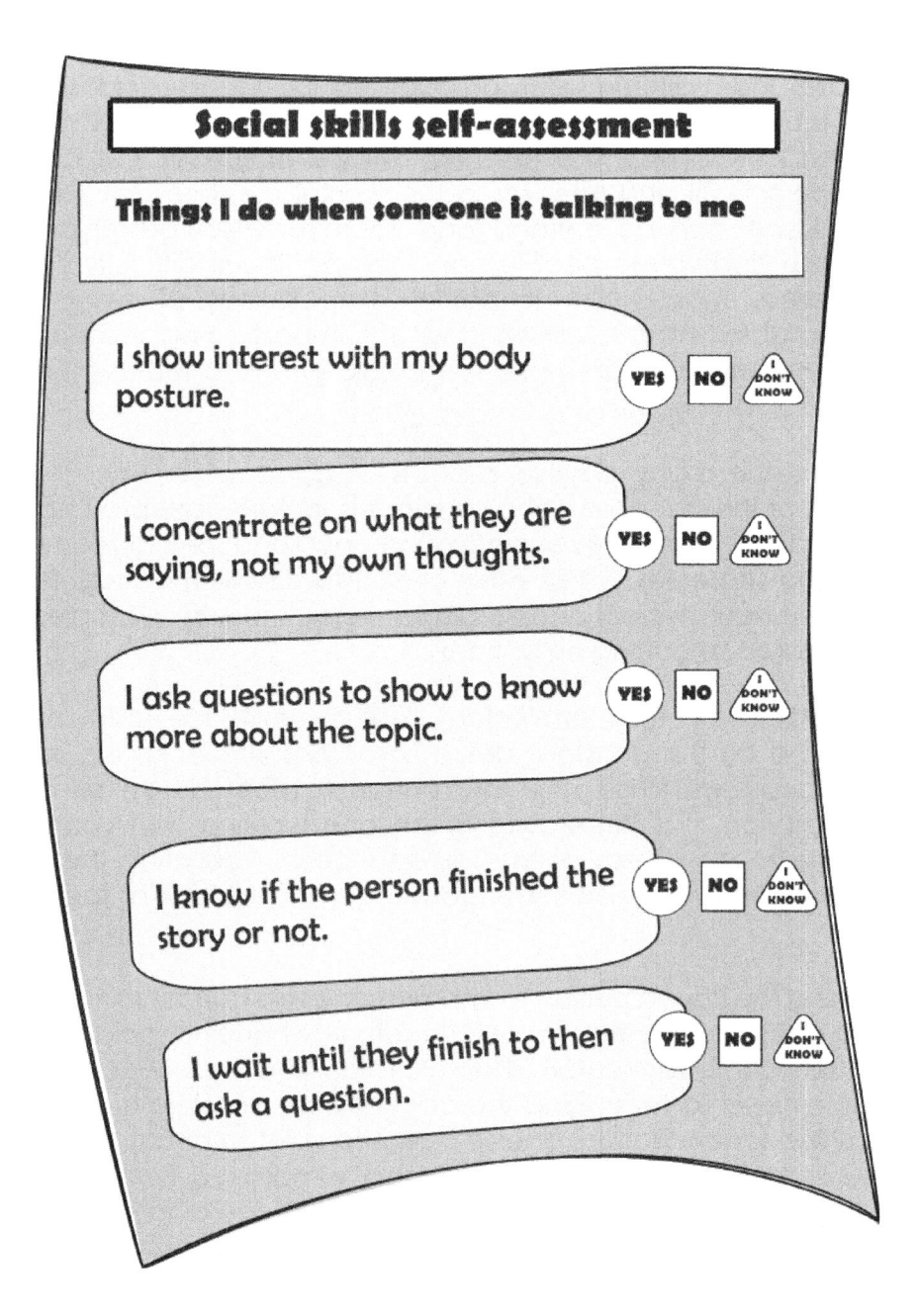

### Social skills self-assessment

**Things I do when someone is talking to me**

I show interest with my body posture. — YES / NO / I DON'T KNOW

I concentrate on what they are saying, not my own thoughts. — YES / NO / I DON'T KNOW

I ask questions to show to know more about the topic. — YES / NO / I DON'T KNOW

I know if the person finished the story or not. — YES / NO / I DON'T KNOW

I wait until they finish to then ask a question. — YES / NO / I DON'T KNOW

Shared resources

# How to use the neurodiversity awareness card game

As I mentioned earlier, the neurodiversity awareness card game includes three types of cards, four cognitive functions, four subsets based on these functions and ten common behaviours, as shown in the diagram below.

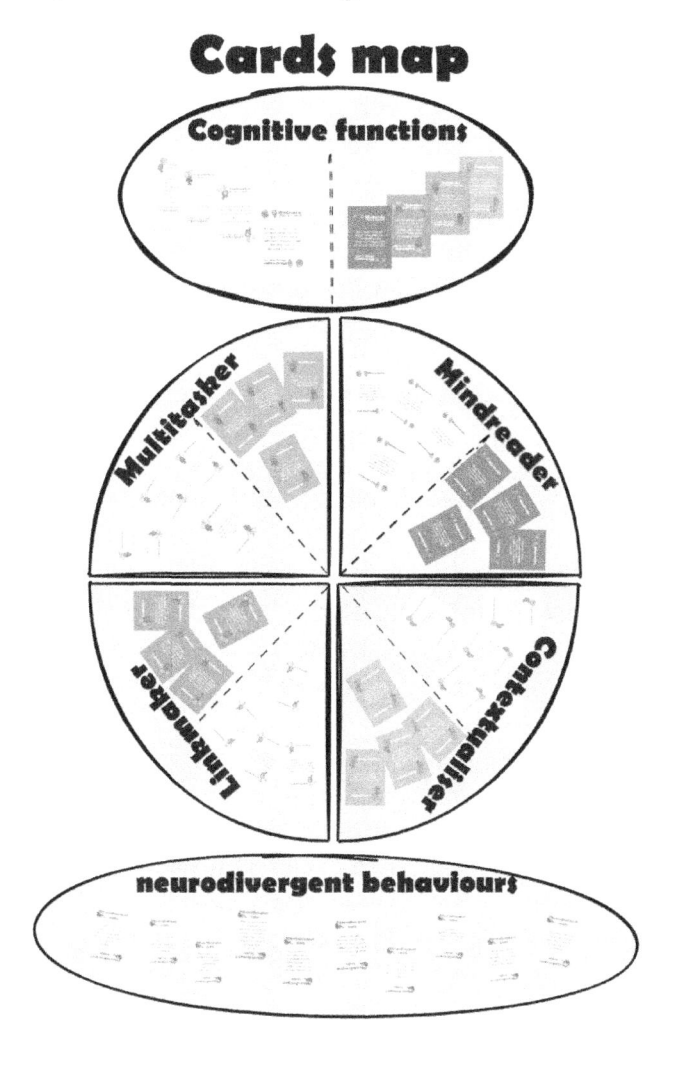

**Cards map**

Cognitive functions

Multitasker | Mindreader

Linksmaker | Contextualiser

neurodivergent behaviours

## How to play 'Me / Not me'

### Start with the subsets

Explain to your young person that this activity is aimed at helping them identify their ways of thinking and behaving. The first part is focused on their thinking processes.

*Step 1*

Hand the Mindreader set to them and ask them to select the cards one by one, starting with the white cards followed by the coloured ones, separating them into two piles: 1) 'This is me' and 2) 'This is not me'. In some cases, you may want to have a third pile for the uncertain ones, which you can revisit later and help them to place in the relevant pile. **Repeat this step with all four subsets. You can choose the order of your preference.**

*Step 2*

Explain to the young person that you will put away the 'This-is-not-me' pile, as these are not relevant to them.

You now have the pile containing all cognitive function descriptions they identify as pursuing. This is also called their '**unique neurodivergent recipe**', or at least a small sample of it. Remind them that no autistic person is the same as another.

*Step 3*

At this point it will make sense to discuss each of the four cognitive functions. Display their recipe by colour, keeping the white cards and coloured cards side by side for each set. Place each definition card above the corresponding pile. Place the Challenges cards alongside the pile of the corresponding colour.

Explain each function in simple terms, using unambiguous language. Explain that these are functions which are important to everyone and many of us face challenges with them to different degrees. However, it is believed that neurodivergent people on the autistic spectrum tend to have more significant challenges with some of them.

Look at their pile, help them analyse what areas they seem to process information and communicate and interact with others and the environment in what is considered a more autistic way.

*Step 4*

The final step is a conversation about how those cognitive functions may explain the roots of their neurodivergent traits and may also have influenced how their personality and life experiences have shaped who they are and how they see themselves (identity and self-esteem).

To support that conversation, you can use the **neurodivergent traits** cards. Read each card with your young person and, similarly to before, ask them to make two piles: one with behaviours they present and one with behaviours they do not present. Once again, keep only the relevant pile and use it to have a conversation about how they feel about each behaviour and how it impacts their lives now, as well as how the behaviours impacted their early years and school life.

The main objective of this part of the conversation is to raise self-awareness in a positive light. Emphasise the concept that all people are different – and different does not mean either right or wrong. Talk about what adjustments are helpful and what situations are unhelpful. Consider having a conversation about masking, check if they are aware of it, how they see it, how they feel about it, if they do mask and the consequences of both, masking and not masking. Do not invalidate their strategies but encourage unmasking.

## Cognitive functions

Cards describing the functions in simple terms, to exemplify ways of thinking.

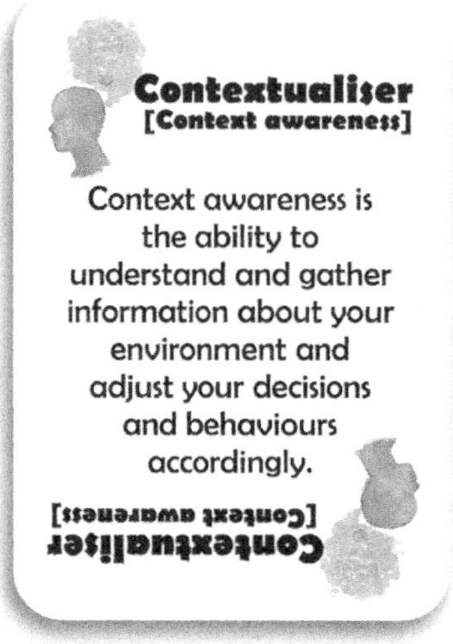

**Contextualiser**
[Context awareness]

Context awareness is the ability to understand and gather information about your environment and adjust your decisions and behaviours accordingly.

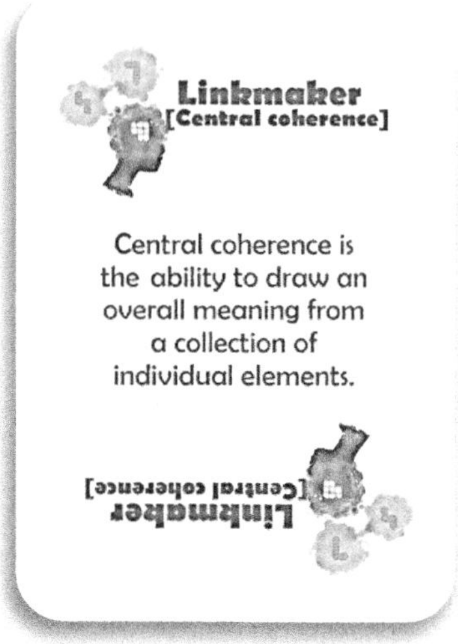

**Linkmaker**
[Central coherence]

Central coherence is the ability to draw an overall meaning from a collection of individual elements.

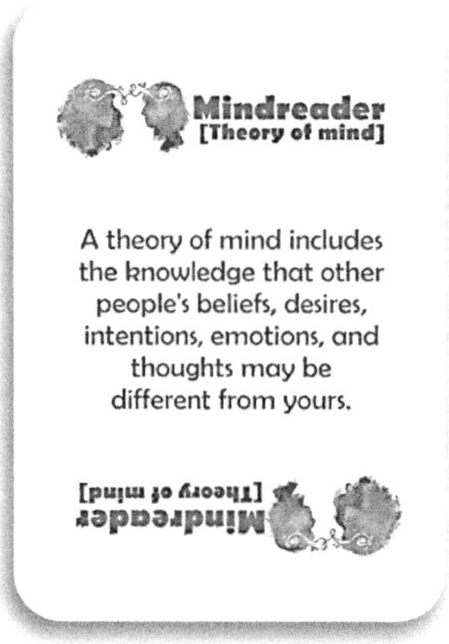

**Mindreader**
[Theory of mind]

A theory of mind includes the knowledge that other people's beliefs, desires, intentions, emotions, and thoughts may be different from yours.

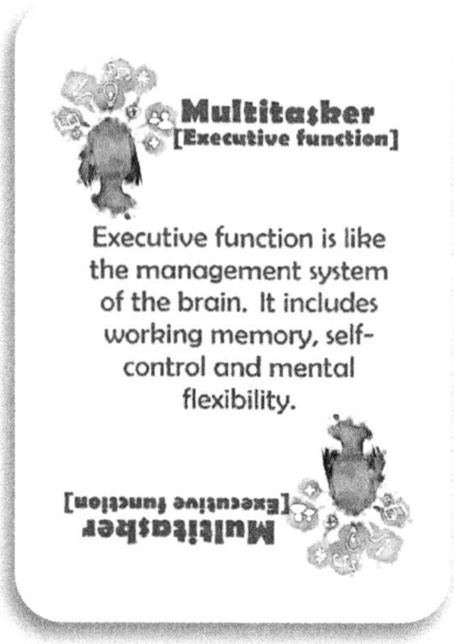

**Multitasker**
[Executive function]

Executive function is like the management system of the brain. It includes working memory, self-control and mental flexibility.

## Cognitive functions

Cards describing the functions to exemplify some difficulties in those areas.

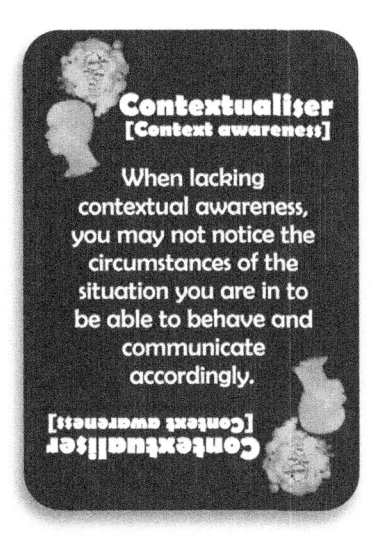

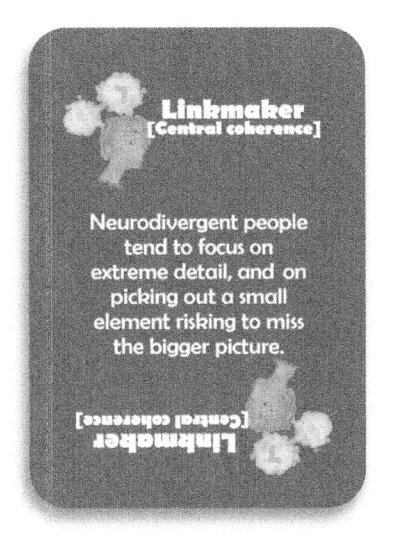

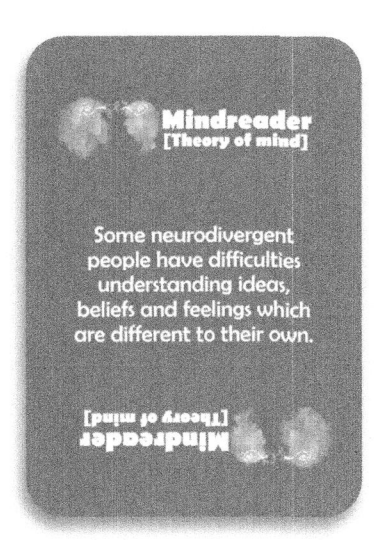

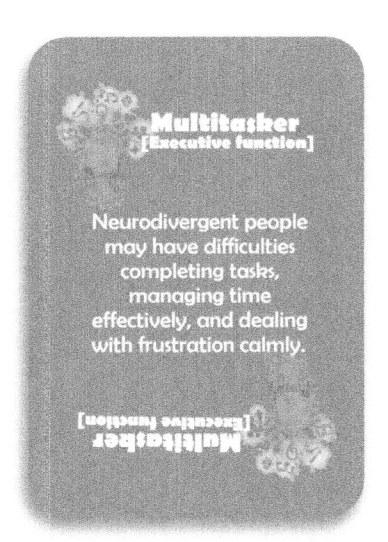

**Contextualiser**
[Context awareness]

When lacking contextual awareness, you may not notice the circumstances of the situation you are in to be able to behave and communicate accordingly.

**Linkmaker**
[Central coherence]

Neurodivergent people tend to focus on extreme detail, and on picking out a small element risking to miss the bigger picture.

**Mindreader**
[Theory of mind]

Some neurodivergent people have difficulties understanding ideas, beliefs and feelings which are different to their own.

**Multitasker**
[Executive function]

Neurodivergent people may have difficulties completing tasks, managing time effectively, and dealing with frustration calmly.

## The Contextualiser

Cards describing stronger contextual awareness.

**Contextualiser**

I enjoy stories and jokes with figurative language, innuendoes and double meanings, as I find them interesting and helpful.

**Contextualiser**

I find it easy to read between the lines when someone is talking to me or when I read something. I can easily see implicit meanings.

**Contextualiser**

I am a good diplomat, because I can guess untold rules, and I can easily adapt to new situations, new groups, new social protocols.

**Contextualiser**

I am extremely good at understanding how the circumstances around an event can affect how facts develop.

## The Contextualiser

Cards describing weaker contextual awareness.

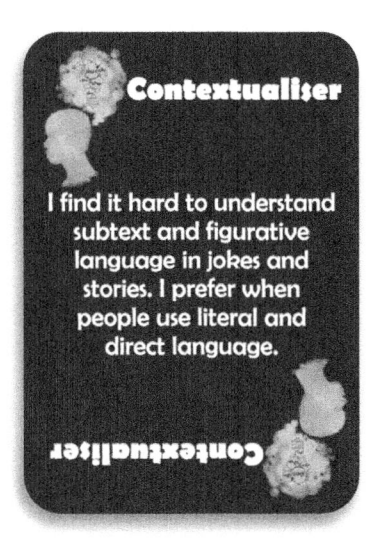

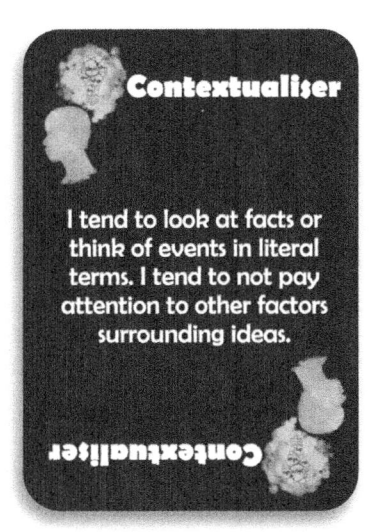

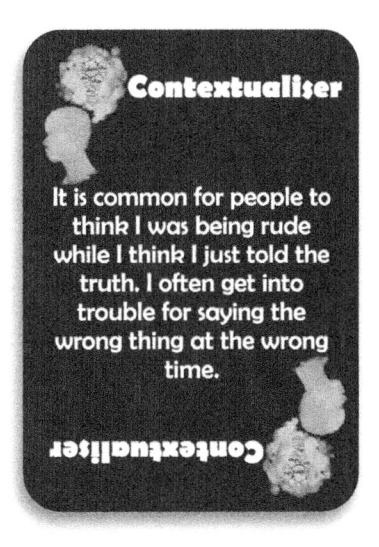

**Contextualiser**

I find it hard to understand subtext and figurative language in jokes and stories. I prefer when people use literal and direct language.

**Contextualiser**

I find it hard to understand unspoken rules, and implicit meanings.

**Contextualiser**

I tend to look at facts or think of events in literal terms. I tend to not pay attention to other factors surrounding ideas.

**Contextualiser**

It is common for people to think I was being rude while I think I just told the truth. I often get into trouble for saying the wrong thing at the wrong time.

**The Tangram Method**

## The Linkmaker

Cards describing stronger central coherence.

---

**Linkmaker**

I can easily link ideas, so I am usually the first to understand a joke, predict the end of a movie or guess the right answer in a charades game.

---

**Linkmaker**

When I visit a new place, I take in the whole area and how it makes me feel without paying attention to the small details.

---

**Linkmaker**

When I read a book or watch a movie, I can get its whole meaning quickly and can easily summarise the plot to someone.

---

**Linkmaker**

I am extremely good at making plans and accurately calculating how long it will take me to complete a task.

Shared resources

## The Linkmaker

Cards describing weaker central coherence.

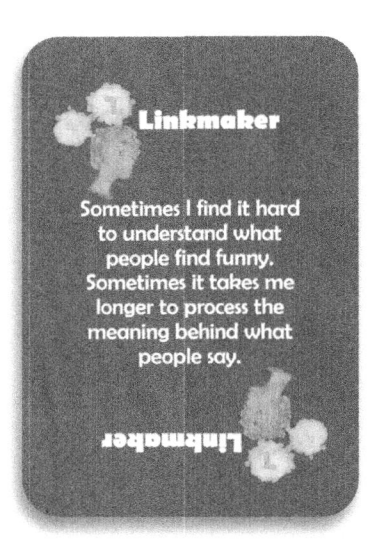

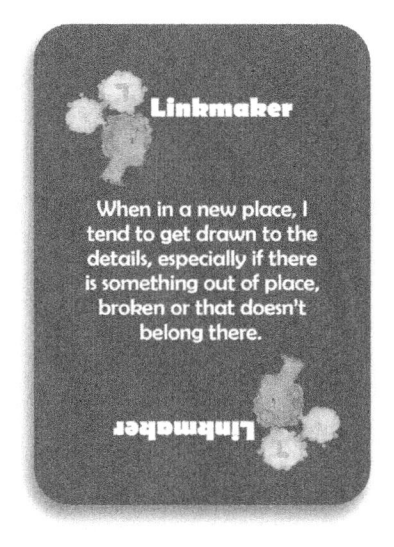

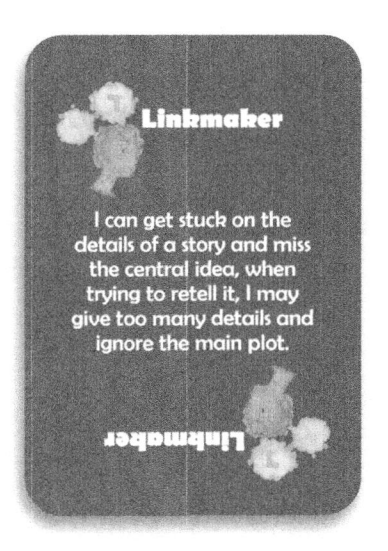

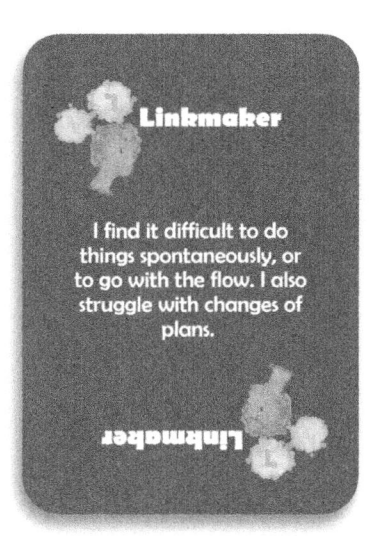

**Linkmaker**
Sometimes I find it hard to understand what people find funny. Sometimes it takes me longer to process the meaning behind what people say.

**Linkmaker**
When in a new place, I tend to get drawn to the details, especially if there is something out of place, broken or that doesn't belong there.

**Linkmaker**
I can get stuck on the details of a story and miss the central idea, when trying to retell it, I may give too many details and ignore the main plot.

**Linkmaker**
I find it difficult to do things spontaneously, or to go with the flow. I also struggle with changes of plans.

## The Mindreader

Cards describing stronger use of the theory of mind.

**Mindreader**
I am incredibly good at understanding other people's minds, how they feel, and what they are thinking about without them telling me.

**Mindreader**
I find social situations fun and easy, so I tend to enjoy being part of a group.

**Mindreader**
When I speak with someone, I can tell by their facial expressions when they are getting bored or when they want to say something.

**Mindreader**
When I read a story or watch a movie, I find it easy to predict the characters' actions and guess their feelings and thoughts.

Shared resources

## The Mindreader

Cards describing weaker use of the theory of mind.

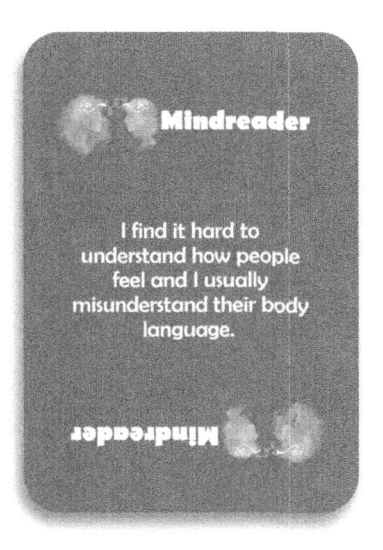

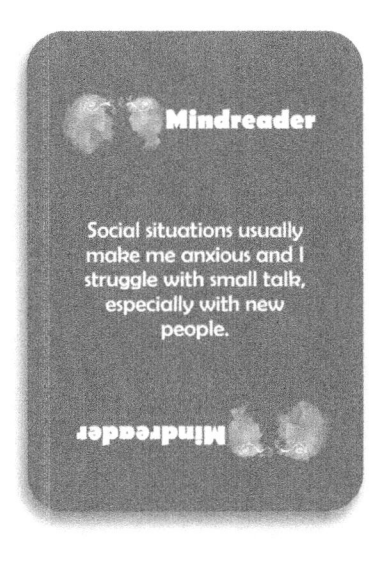

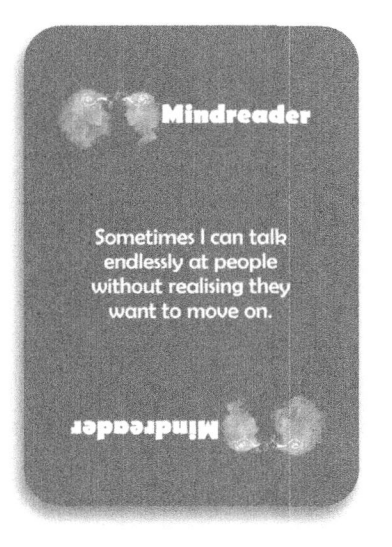

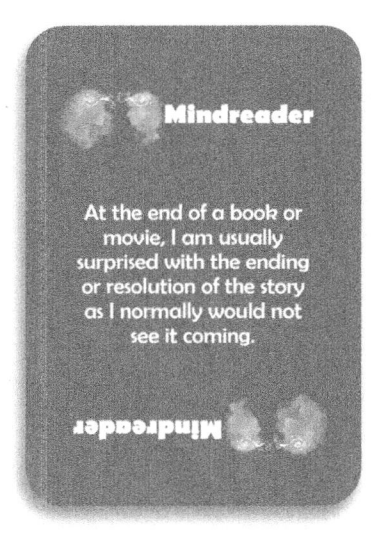

---

**Mindreader**

I find it hard to understand how people feel and I usually misunderstand their body language.

---

**Mindreader**

Social situations usually make me anxious and I struggle with small talk, especially with new people.

---

**Mindreader**

Sometimes I can talk endlessly at people without realising they want to move on.

---

**Mindreader**

At the end of a book or movie, I am usually surprised with the ending or resolution of the story as I normally would not see it coming.

### The Tangram Method

## The Multitasker

Cards describing stronger use of executive function.

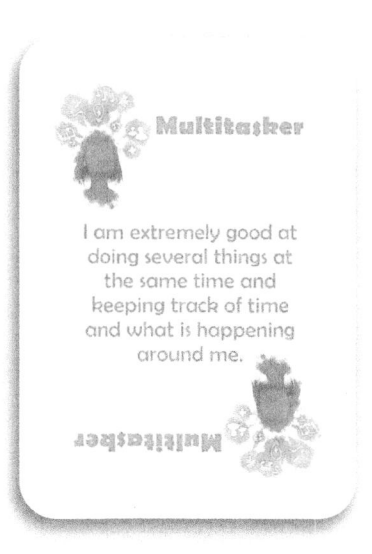

**Multitasker**
I can easily adapt to new places, new people, situations, new rules, and new routines. I always find changes exciting and easy.

**Multitasker**
If someone interrupts me, I can pause what I am doing for a while and then switch back to it easily.

**Multitasker**
I have a wide range of interests but sometimes I lose interest in some of them and move on because I am always finding new interests.

**Multitasker**
I am extremely good at doing several things at the same time and keeping track of time and what is happening around me.

Shared resources

## The Multitasker

Cards describing weaker use of executive function.

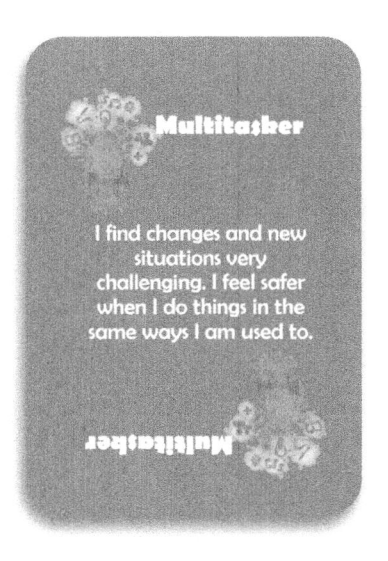

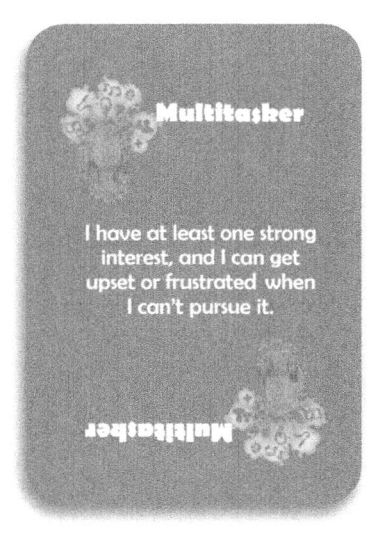

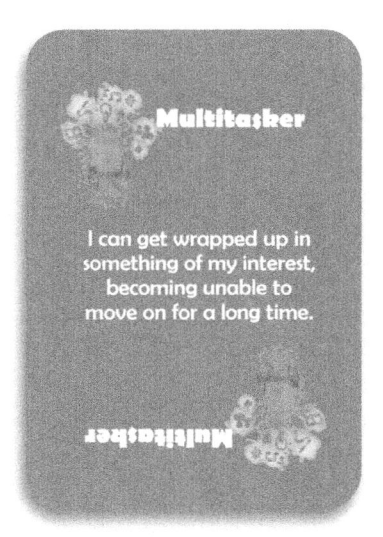

**Multitasker**
I find changes and new situations very challenging. I feel safer when I do things in the same ways I am used to.

**Multitasker**
I can get stuck on small details, like something missing or out of place. Sometimes I cannot move on until I fix or complaint about it.

**Multitasker**
I have at least one strong interest, and I can get upset or frustrated when I can't pursue it.

**Multitasker**
I can get wrapped up in something of my interest, becoming unable to move on for a long time.

## The Tangram Method

### Neurodivergent traits

Cards describing some common traits.

---

**Neurodivergent traits**

When I am overwhelmed by sensory or cognitive stimuli, I may have a shutdown or meltdown.

---

**Neurodivergent traits**

When I am overwhelmed by sensory or cognitive overload, I may do or say repetitive things (stimming).

---

**Neurodivergent traits**

When I try to look people in the eye, I can get distracted and end up interrupting the flow of the conversation.

---

**Neurodivergent traits**

When someone asks me a question or explains something to me, I may take longer than most people to process it and respond or react.

## Shared resources

**Neurodivergent traits**

I can become non-verbal in certain situations or with some people, and usually I cannot stop this from happening.

**Neurodivergent traits**

I normally speak frankly and directly without filters, unless I think carefully and plan ahead on what to say.

**Neurodivergent traits**

I usually prefer to eat the same food every day. There are foods that I refuse to try as I know I dislike them.

**Neurodivergent traits**

I can become vocal or upset if I see injustice happening or things done in the wrong way.

**The Tangram Method**

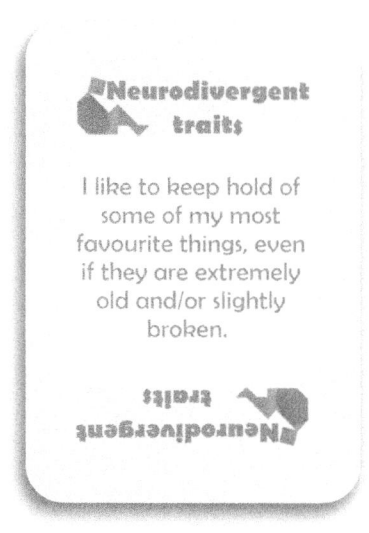

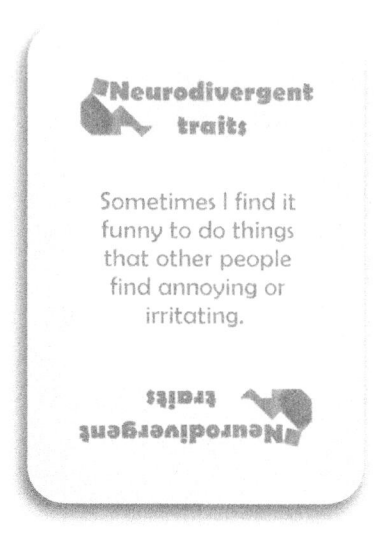

> **Neurodivergent traits**
>
> I like to keep hold of some of my most favourite things, even if they are extremely old and/or slightly broken.

> **Neurodivergent traits**
>
> Sometimes I find it funny to do things that other people find annoying or irritating.

It is important to remember that these cards are purely conversation prompts as opposed to prescriptions or rigid conceptualisations. They are not exhaustive either.

Using the cards to start to raise self-awareness and strengthen a sense of self is the main point. Theorising about autism or any other neurodivergent label is not covered by this method. The main task is to open up the dialogue and start grasping concepts as a means to make informed decisions about what to do next, what further searches the young person may want to pursue. Moreover, the cards are a simple device to make these concepts more tangible and to promote the idea of being different being normal. It is not only OK to be different, it is *normal* to be different.

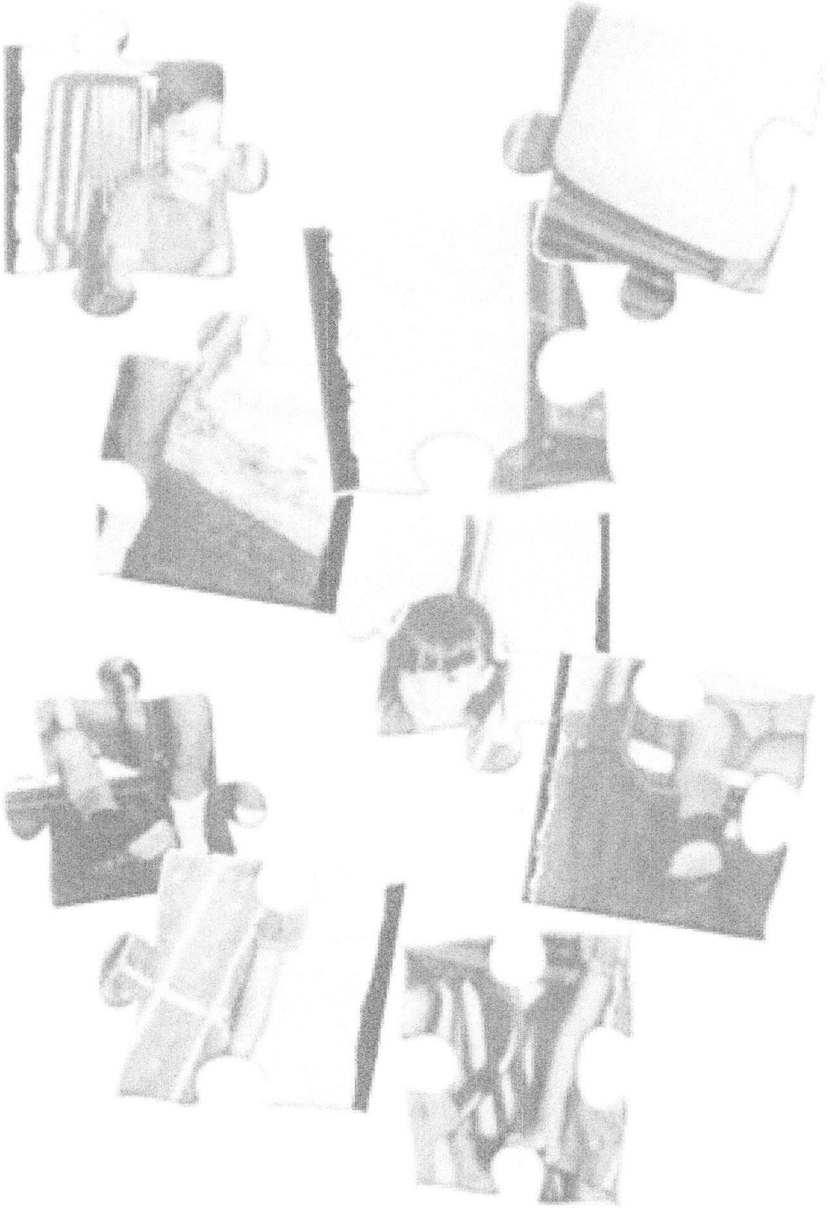

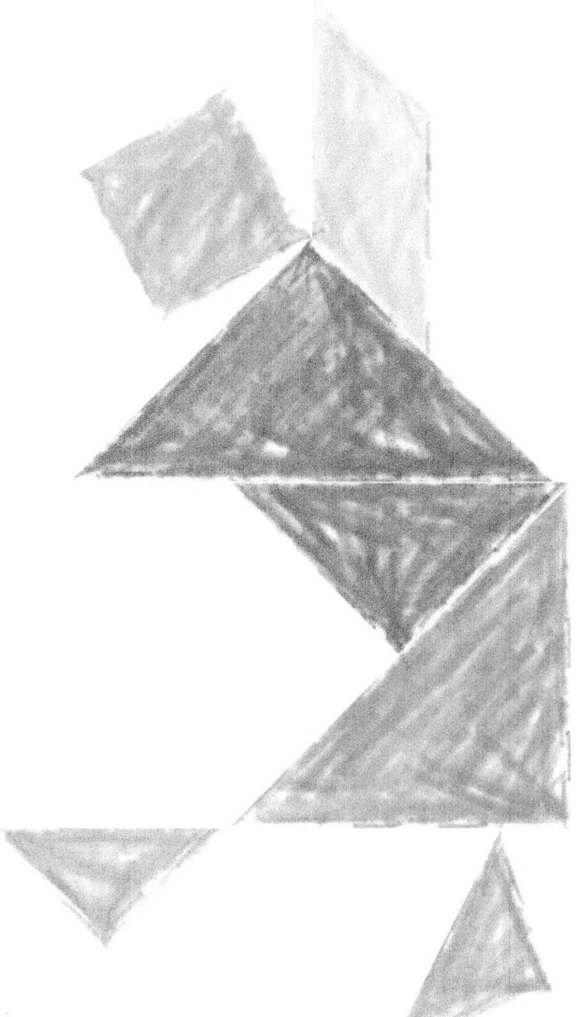

# Extended resources and final thoughts

I started this book talking about how I identify as a learner and storyteller. These two characteristics are intrinsically intertwined because storytelling is one of the most ancient ways through which humanity has shared knowledge with younger generations; the most significant learning experiences encompass many stories to be told.

Storytelling is a generous way of sharing knowledge and wisdom, as much as it is entertaining and a meaningful way to connect with others. As I reach the final chapter of the story of the Tangram Method, I want to share a collection of pointers to resources available online via various websites, including my own, as well as my academic publications. I hope these resources can support you in fostering self-awareness and self-worth in neurodivergent young people. I have listed resources available in my personal webspace but also included a list of publications I have referred to over time when seeking knowledge, information or inspiration.

I am aware that we live in an era where it is easy to find information about anything just by typing a question into a search engine. However, I value recommendations from people I know and respect; and I have benefitted from curated information many times. For that reason, I want to offer you the same as I have been given. My references list is not exhaustive but contains some key texts.

## Materials available via *Inclusive Thoughts*

*Inclusive Thoughts* is a blog in constant transformation that I started in 2006 as my research journal. Originally it was private and the only other person to have access to it apart from me was my supervisor. After completing my studies in 2011, I made it partially public. Since then, the blog has been refocused from its original purpose to embracing a sort of continuous metamorphosis. As part of my opening this conversation about the Tangram Method, I have made some resources available in a page dedicated to this book.

## Supplementary resources

The neurodiversity awareness cards are available online in pdf format ready for printing, but they can also be found for purchase as a finished product.

In additional to the cards presented in the book, I have also produced some communication cards which can be found online, ready for printing and also available as finished products.

As a follow-up to this book, I have now completed a handbook with activities that can be photocopied and printed out to be used alongside the method. The book also brings all the cards, ready to be photocopied.

The best place to find all the above is my website, **Inclusive Thoughts** at hilravinha.com.

## Some earlier publications

### Contribution to a phenomenal book

Vinha, H.G. (2020). Siblings Belonging Together. In *Belonging for People with Profound Intellectual and Multiple Disabilities* (pp. 77–80). Routledge.

### Collaboration with Professor Mel Nind as a result of the project about quality in inclusive research

Nind, M. & Vinha, H. (2016). Creative interactions with data: using visual and metaphorical devices in repeated focus groups. *Qualitative Research* 16 (1) 9–2

Nind, M. & Vinha, H. (2015). Quality and capacity in inclusive research with people with learning disabilities, UK Data Archive.

Nind, M. & Vinha, H. (2014). Doing research inclusively: bridges to multiple possibilities in inclusive research. *British Journal of Learning Disabilities* 42 (2) 102–109

Nind, M. & Vinha, H. (2013). Building an inclusive research community: the challenges and benefits. *Learning Disability Today*.

Nind, M. & Vinha, H. (2013). Practical considerations in doing research inclusively and doing it well: lessons for inclusive researchers. NCRM.

Nind, M. & Vinha, H. (2012). Doing research inclusively, doing research well? Report of the study: quality and capacity in inclusive research with people with learning disabilities. University of Southampton.

Nind, M. & Vinha, H. (2012). Doing research inclusively, doing research well? University of Southampton.

## PhD thesis and some articles of the time

Vinha, M.H.G.L. (2011). Learners' perspectives of identity and difference: a narrative study on the visual and verbal representation of self and other. University of Southampton.

Vinha, H.G. (2009). Enabling findings: making research findings accessible by using literary structure. [ethnographic fiction]

Vinha, H.G. (2009). The exceptional experience of difference.

Vinha, H.G. (2009). Why I am doing this in this way: a reflective narrative.

## Book review: the first publication in the UK

Vinha, H.G. (2006). Book review. Researching life stories: method, theory and analyses in a biographical age. *International Journal of Research and Method in Education 29 (2) 259–264*

Extended resources and final thoughts

# A final thought

I dedicated this book to him, so it is fair to let you know a little more about Sessé. When I was two years old, I was given the present of a baby brother with physical disabilities, with a developmental delay and severe autism. When he was born, an advocate-sister was also born.

In this picture he is sitting on a chair because he had not learned to stand up or walk yet. At that time, I used to take him with me to play outside with my friends. Sometimes I would carry him on my tricycle which conveniently had a back seat.

Until he learned to walk at the age of four, on many occasions, even though he was almost the same size as me, I would sometimes carry him in my arms, which he found amusing and hilarious. He also enjoyed the fact that other people passing by would find it funny.

**153**

**The Tangram Method**

In adolescence, when he had been long able to walk, sometimes he would remember the fun of being carried around and would refuse to walk back home from our street after playtime. How much fun it was (for him) to be carried by me, now with the help of my loyal friend Umberto. Although, on occasions we used questionable approaches to persuade him to walk.

He is full of cheeky ways to get his wishes met. He is also sensitive and caring, with an extraordinary ability to read my mind even if he cannot articulate a full sentence using words but can say so much with his eyes, his kisses, hugs, tears and laughter. That is probably why I never minded carrying him (literally) and continued to do so (in my heart) everywhere I went.

Nowadays we live far apart, still, he is with me in everything I do. Such as when writing this book. My entire life has been touched and influenced by his life and by the strong bond we developed over the years.

That is why I care about people with a learning disability or any form of difference that can deem them excluded. *Inclusive Thoughts* is the name of my blog and is also the way I think. Inclusion is more than a cause, it is part of who I am, it is in my blood.

# **Acknowledgements**

As I write these words of thankfulness, I feel a deep sense of gratitude for the path that has led me to this very moment. From my earliest memories, I have harboured a deep love for the intricate dance of language, a passion ignited by the beauty and power of words. When I was eleven years old, a magical moment occurred. The moment my father presented me with a typewriter was truly a defining one. This desired machine symbolised my aspirations and desires. That simple machine became my portal to a world where my imagination soared, igniting a passion for sharing stories and expressing myself through words.

I have been fortunate enough to complete a doctoral research and write a thesis that I am still proud of. I then collaborated with and contributed to academic publications, including a phenomenal book in which I tell the story of my growing up together with my little brother and the impact of his disability on our young lives. Having now completed this book, I am humbled by the countless individuals who have played a role in bringing this idea to fruition. To each and every one who has offered support, guidance, encouragement and inspiration along the way, I offer my deepest and most heartfelt thanks. This book would not exist without their belief in me and their invaluable contribution to its creation, which I try to put into words here.

To my friend and former research supervisor, Professor Melanie Nind, who believed in me right from the start. Melanie not only opened the first and most significant door for me but also provided invaluable academic and personal support. Her influence on my research, endorsing the integration of creativity and storytelling into my thesis is present throughout this book.

To Weaver Lima, for accepting the challenge of illustrating my data-collection materials and exceeding all my expectations by skilfully transforming some of my data into captivating cartoon strips, which I incorporated within this book.

To Dr Roger Jones, who has been an inspiration and role model, making a significant contribution to my learning about neurodiversity and for becoming a friend for life with lovely Peter.

To Ana Beatriz Benigno for her imaginative art, translating cognitive functions into beautiful watercolour illustrations for the neurodiversity card game. She also brought to life the stages of the Relate model.

To Tom Smith whose life experience was pivotal in initiating me into the enriching realm of autism awareness. My gratitude extends to Tom's parents and grandparents, exemplary role models and dedicated supporters, whose contributions have been instrumental in fostering not only Tom's growth but also my professional development.

To Lewis Clark-Dowden, for educating me about being neurodivergent through his lived experience, over the years turning into a close friend. He planted the original seed that later blossomed into the Tangram Method.

## Acknowledgements

To Michael and Elizabeth Dacombe for their contribution to my work, grounded in mutual trust and respect, which rendered them the perfect first readers of my manuscript, an invaluable contribution for which I am forever thankful.

To James Dacombe for sharing his intellectual prowess with me and consistently challenging and propelling my own growth. James's openness in expressing his thoughts and experiences was a crucial source of insight for the conceptualisation and the emergence of the ideas that developed into this book.

To Tegan Longcroft for teaching me about the delicate beauty of neurodivergent brilliance.

To Logan Kruger for his openness and honesty in sharing his perceptions and ideas about a world neurotypically nonsensical.

To Jackson Leonard for teaching me the splendour of thinking differently and being artistic and original in a world full of boxes to contain people.

To Jamie Windibank for helping me reflect on the absence of labels and how we build our own road by walking.

To my chosen brother, Umberto Lima Soares, who has been part of my life since childhood, who embraced Sessé and his cheeky demands (including to be carried when he did not fancy walking back home) who continues to share crucial moments of life with me. His constant unconditional and certain love means the world to me.

**The Tangram Method**

To Adriana Fernandes and Regina Camara for all they taught me in my initial teaching years and for becoming my sisters and my safe place since.

To Gilcilene Luz, Ana Debora Pessoa and Ivone Melo for the friendship since our first year at university, followed by decades of shared laughter, tears, arguments, reconciliations and everything in between. For the amazing experience of growing wiser and older together while living oceans apart.

To Ewelina Szulc and Jay Bak for becoming family years ago and, more recently, Jay for providing helpful feedback after reading this manuscript.

To Linda Kirkham for believing in my work, supporting me in my best and worst days by being my rock.

To Michael Heppell, whose mentorship fostered the evolution of an embryonic idea into a tangible reality, this book, and for creating such a brilliant collective of authors which has been central towards getting this project over the line.

To my family, for their abundant love and encouragement, above all my husband, Rod Campbell and his unwavering support at every step of the way, allowing me to reference him endlessly as a neurodivergent example and role model for the young people who helped me develop the Tangram Method.

# References and further reading

## References

Baron-Cohen, S., et al. (2001). The autism-spectrum quotient (AQ): evidence from Asperger syndrome/high-functioning autism, males and females, scientists and mathematicians. Journal of Autism and Developmental Disorders, 31(1), 5–17.

Bettelheim, B. (1967). The empty fortress: infantile autism and the birth of the self (1st Free Press pbk. ed). Free Press.

Gernsbacher, M. A., et al. (2018). Do puzzle pieces and autism puzzle piece logos evoke negative associations?. Autism : the international journal of research and practice, 22(2), 118–125.

Goffman, E. (1959). The presentation of self in everyday life. Anchor Books, Doubleday.

Grossberg, B. (2012). Asperger's rules!: how to make sense of school and friends. Magination Press.

Jung, C. G., & Beebe, J. (2017). Psychological types. Routledge.

Lecheler, M., et al. (2021). A Matter of Perspective: An Exploratory Study of a Theory of Mind Autism Intervention for Adolescents. Psychological Reports, 124(1), 39-53.

## References and further reading

Lukito, S., et al. (2017). Specificity of executive function and theory of mind performance in relation to attention-deficit/hyperactivity symptoms in autism spectrum disorders. Molecular Autism, 8(1), 1–13.

Malik, G. (2013). Existentialism and Classroom Practice. IOSR Journal of Humanities and Social Science, 8, 87-91.

Shaul, J. & Klaw, R. (2009). Ryuu the game: using a fantasy world of dragons to build social skills in humans

Singer, J. (2017). Neurodiversity: the birth of an idea. ISBN: 978-0648154709

Vygotsky, L. S. (1962). Thought and language (E. Hanfmann & G. Vakar, Eds.). M.I.T. Press, Massachusetts Institute of Technology.

Whitmore, J. (2017). Coaching for performance: the principles and practice of coaching and leadership (Fifth edition). Nicholas Brealey Publishing.

## Further reading

Attwood, T. (2015). The complete guide to Asperger's syndrome (Revised edition). Jessica Kingsley Publishers.

Barton, M. (2014). A Different Kettle of Fish: a Day in the Life of a Physics Student with Autism. Jessica Kingsley Publishers. http://site.ebrary.com/id/10861443.

BARTON, M. (2021). IT'S RAINING CATS AND DOGS: an autism spectrum guide to the confusing world of idioms,... metaphors and everyday expressions. JESSICA KINGSLEY.

Barton, M. (2022). What has autism ever done for us?: how the autistic way of thinking revolutionised the world.

Blackbyrn, S. (2022). The OSKAR Coaching Model: The definite Guide.

Ekins, E. (2021). Queerly autistic: the ultimate guide for LGBTQIA+ teens on the spectrum. Jessica Kingsley Publishers.
Freire, Paulo. 1996. 'Pedagogy of the Oppressed', 164.

Goodall, E., et al. (2016). The Autism Spectrum Guide to Sexuality and Relationships: Understand Yourself and Make Choices that are Right for You. Jessica Kingsley Publishers.

Grandin, T., & Moore, D. (2021). Navigating autism: 9 mindsets for helping kids on the spectrum (First edition). W.W. Norton & Company.

Grandin, T., & Panek, R. (2013). The autistic brain: thinking across the spectrum. Houghton Mifflin Harcourt.

Grandin, T., & Scariano, M. (1996). Emergence: labeled autistic: a true story. Grand Central Publishing.

Humanmetrics (nd). Personality test based on Jung and Briggs Myers typology. https://www.humanmetrics.com/personality

Johnson, M., & Wintgens, A. (2016). The selective mutism resource manual (Second edition). Routledge.

Myers, I. B., & Myers, P. B. (2010). Gifts differing: understanding personality type. Davies-Black.

O'Toole, J. C. (2012). The Asperkid's (secret) book of social rules: the handbook of not-so-obvious social guidelines for tweens and teens with Asperger syndrome (10th anniversary edition). Jessica Kingsley Publishers.

O'Toole, J. C. (2013). The Asperkid's Launch Pad: Home Design to Empower Everyday Superheroes.

### References and further reading

Papadopoulos, R. K. (2012). The Handbook of Jungian Psychology: Theory, Practice and Applications. Taylor and Francis.

Sterling, L. (nd). The Social Survival Guide for Teens on the Autism Spectrum: How to Make Friends and Navigate Your Emotions.

Thomas Armstrong. (2021). The power of neurodiversity: unleashing the advantages of your differently wired brain. Da Capo Lifelong Books.

Wells, J. (2022). Wired differently: 30 neurodiverse people who you should know. Jessica Kingsley Publishers.

Wharmby, P. (2024). UNTYPICAL PB: How the world isn't built for autistic people and what we should all do about it. Mudlark.

I always wanted to go back to my thesis and turn it into a book accessible beyond academia, to reach teachers, parents and young people. Maybe I will still do that one day.

Meanwhile, I made it available as a printed book, to share my attempt to weave narrative, visuals and data into one piece of research.

There is a copy that resides on a shelf at the Hartley library (and the copy in my supervisor's office, I hope) and a pdf on the eprints repository. (https://eprints.soton.ac.uk/192459/).

I recently translated it to Portuguese and made it available as an ebook, so my family and friends in Brazil can access it.

# References and further reading

**Siblings Belonging Together**

BY Hilra Gondim Vinha in

Belonging for People with Profound Intellectual and Multiple Disabilities: Pushing the Boundaries of Inclusion.

Edited By Melanie Nind & Iva Strnadová

First Published 2020
Imprint Routledge
eBook ISBN9780429260711/9780429260711
https://doi.org/10.4324/9780429260711

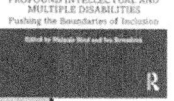

## The Tangram Method

**The Tangram Method** is an innovative approach inspired by the ancient puzzle and shaped by the voices of neurodivergent young people. This transformative book offers a practical framework for meaningful conversations that unlock deeper understanding, raise self-awareness and encourage the unmasking of autism.

Through engaging stories and practical insights, you will discover the seven key principles that form the foundation of the **Tangram Method**, each represented by a unique character inspired by real neurodivergent young people.

This book is for

* educators, therapists and social workers working with young people across various settings,

* parents and caregivers seeking to improve their understanding and to better support their children.

# References and further reading

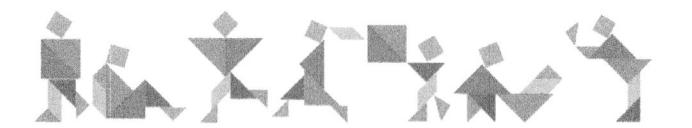

Printed in Great Britain
by Amazon